DOLLS
OF THE
WORLD

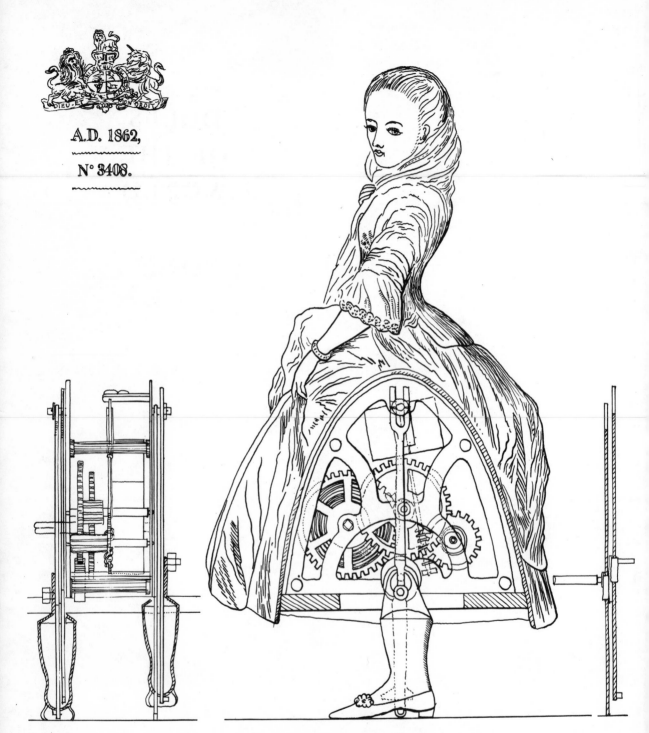

Mechanical doll, 1862, U.S.A., with British Specification patent

DOLLS
OF THE
WORLD

GWEN WHITE

Mills & Boon
London

*

*Written and illustrated by the
same author:*

Ancient and Modern Dolls
Toys' Adventures at the Zoo
Ladybird, Ladybird
A Book of Toys
Eight Little Frogs
A Book of Dolls
A Book of Pictorial Perspective
A World of Pattern

*

*Printed in Great Britain by
W. S. Cowell Ltd, Butter Market, Ipswich
from plates drawn by the author
and published by Mills & Boon
Grafton Way, London*

INTRODUCTION

It is difficult to decide what a true doll is, the very beginning of the word DOLL being rather obscure. Some say that it comes from 'idol', but hardly any of the dolls which I have found are worshipped as such. Those in which the spirits of ancestors rest are reverenced, and those used by witch-doctors are held in awe. Also there are fertility symbols and protective charms.

As with many other things, the more one finds out about dolls the more there is to know, and in tracking their history, all kinds of interesting items are unearthed at the same time.

The first dolls may have been stones picked up from the ground, which in a vague way suggested the shape of a baby, and could be hugged, or laid down on the grass to sleep. The early doll from California is similar to a stone. A stick, also, might suggest something. In Poland there are the queer witches' sticks, and in Australia forked sticks make do for a doll, when someone is pretending to carry a baby. So, from a stone, we may get the clay-modelled dolls, and, from a stick, dolls of carved wood.

What does a face matter, or even arms and legs, to a child with an imagination? A block of wood can be a man or a woman at will, it can stand up or lie down. Many English Pedlar Dolls had no legs, and many dolls have neither arms nor legs. There are the German Stump dolls, Russian Nest dolls, Tumbler dolls from all parts of the world, and the clay dolls from the Gran Chaco, which have no arms for fear of breaking. Usually hands seem more important than feet. Sometimes a doll will have quite well-made hands, yet underneath her clothes may be nothing but two wooden stumps, or even a forked twig.

Faces, when they have them, show what is considered beautiful in that particular country. There are flat faces, wide noses, big eyes, small ears, long necks, in fact endless differences, but all are trying to look beautiful, for not often does a doll set out to be ugly. A modern American doll, 'Poor Pitiful Pearl', is doing her best to get away from the conventional film-star beauty, and is a change from many a present-day doll with goo-goo eyes and a cute expression.

Although many of the hand-carved wooden dolls of the European peasants are gradually disappearing, and plastic dolls are taking their place, these in turn are seen alongside beautifully made 'rag-dolls', with embroidered features, and hand-made clothes in the manner of dolls of the 16th century showing regional costumes. The extraordinary workmanship which goes into the making of playthings is almost unbelievable, and the history of dolls goes so far back into the past that, in some cases, the reason for their being has been lost in obscurity.

It is one thing to search for dolls and make sketches of them, and quite another to put them in some order. Historical or geographical, which should it be? and yet how can one be separated from the other? Dolls have been known as 'Messengers of Peace', so from a Doll's point of view, political divisions count as nothing, and the world is just one big place.

A few of these little figures may never have been intended as playthings, and today some dolls are made primarily as ornaments, but in the main the dolls here are true dolls, that is they can be played with and carried about. Others have crept in which, although not toys, will surely interest children and grown-ups, just as they have delighted me while making the drawings for this picture book.

GWEN WHITE, A.R.C.A.

CONTENTS

*

ILLUSTRATIONS IN THE TEXT

PLATES IN COLOUR AND BLACK-AND-WHITE

(Page numbers of colour plates in heavy type)

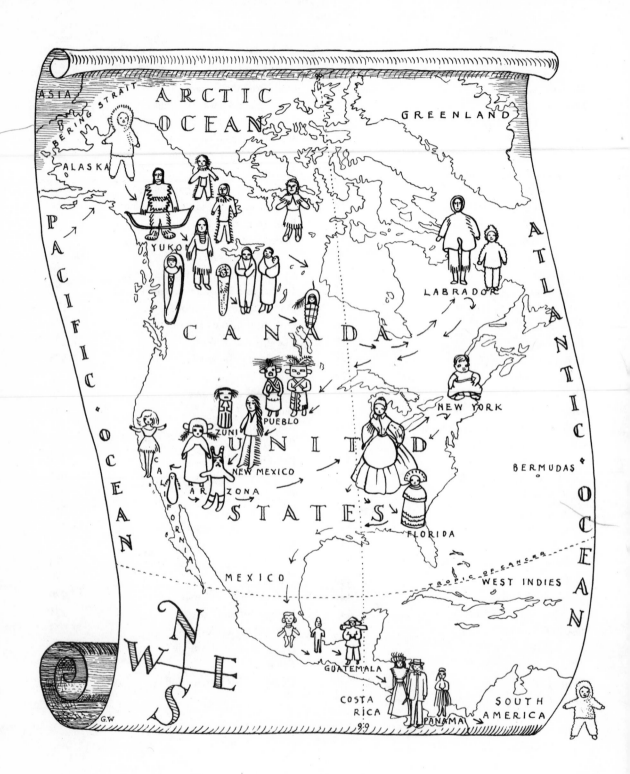

DOLLS OF NORTH AMERICA

Here, in the far north, dolls have been found in the graves of children, just as they have been in other parts of the world. In Alaska the natives build small wooden houses and put dolls on the graves, together with a cross. These houses are painted in bright colours, and inside they put tiny tables, complete with dishes, pots and pans, and even sewing materials. This custom is similar to that found in ancient Egypt and in Greece, but in those countries the little objects were put in the grave with the child, and not in small houses on the surface.

The boys play with marbles, kites, and roller skates, the girls with dolls, and the little ones play with furry dolls, rather like teddy bears. The girls will sit on the floor in their homes and cut out clothes for their dolls, small dickies and trousers just like those the people have worn for years and years with no change in the fashion. In the evenings the dolls are undressed, laid on a scrap of deerskin on a toy wooden bed, and covered with a quilt.

These dolls are furry, and modern dolls are dressed in felt and pieces of fur in the same manner. Often a cardboard face or one of buckram is stitched into the fur hood rather like a mask. The features are painted, and if the face is of wood they will be carved.

The Eskimo children as far away as East Greenland have dolls. Some are carved from bones, others may be from whales' teeth or from stones. They are scraped and scrubbed into shape with hard flints, and the carved features have high cheekbones and broad flat noses.

Dolls have been found which are extra tall, and some from near the Bering Straits have had eyes of tin or ivory. The fathers usually make the dolls, and the children dress them in Eskimo clothes; but they do not always have dolls, and they may make do with mere bundles of rags or scraps of sealskin, tied with thongs at the waist and neck, and with no features visible to a grown-up.

The mothers carry their children about in their hoods, but a child does not have a hood of her own until she is old enough to get married. A small girl will borrow her mother's hood, tuck her doll into it, and copy the curious swaying movement of her mother as she walks.

Some of the dolls are used as charms and as a protection from spirits, when the natives are hunting for seals, and others are fastened to the kayaks to prevent accidents.

Sometimes modern dolls are brought on the whaling ships, fair-haired ones from shops, and even precious scraps of flannel are used for dressing them; these will be tucked into the hoods with the native dolls.

A belief among some of the American Indians is that when a baby dies, it is too weak to find its way alone to Paradise, so the mother must help it until it is strong enough to make the journey by itself. She ties a lock of the baby's hair with paper and coloured ribbons, and with its playthings, amulets and clothes, she makes a large bundle which she ties up in a criss-cross fashion like a traditional bambino. Treated almost as a real baby, this bundle is laid in the empty cradle by the fireside, carried about on journeys, given presents at festivals, and this is continued until the baby is considered old enough to reach Paradise on its own.

Among some of the tribes of North America, a mother who has lost her child will sometimes fill the cradle with black feathers and quills, and this she will carry about for even a year or more, talking to it as if a real baby lay there. The Chippewa Indians do much the same thing, only they fashion the feathers into the shape of a child before laying them in the cradle.

The dolls of the American Indian children are made of wood and covered with felt. They are strong and fairly heavy to hold; dressed in coloured rugs, there are men dolls and women dolls with often a baby doll tucked in the rug at the back. Some have wooden legs, and others may have a mere block of wood so that they can stand up.

✳   ✳   ✳

A very different kind of doll is made by the Seminole tribe. These people live in Florida, the married sons living with their wives' families. The women are very fond of sewing, and nearly everyone of them possesses a sewing-machine.

The dolls are made from palmetto fibre, the darkish brown colour being suitable for the faces, hands and feet. Palmetto is the name given to the several varieties of small palm which grow in the southern states of North America.

The Seminole dresses are carefully copied for the dolls, and are made up of brightly coloured pieces of cloth. Long even strips are cut from various coloured lengths of material and stitched together again by machining. This is cut again, sometimes at right angles, and sometimes on the cross, i.e. diagonally, and these strips are sewn together again, thus making patterns, more and more complicated, depending on how many times the material is cut and joined. The dolls are made in various sizes, and the price is according to the size. (25 cents to $3.50 in 1958.)

✳   ✳   ✳

The Hopi and the Zuñi tribes live in the Indian Reservations in north-eastern Arizona and New Mexico, by the side of the Navajo and Apache tribes.

The Hopi villages are built on sandstone plateaux, and the people believe that their gods, the Kachinas, live in the snow and ice of the high San Francisco peaks. They believe that the gods borrow the bodies of living men and come down to the villages to distribute presents and to receive prayers. They, the gods, are mainly to do with the control of the weather, and especially the bringing of rain.

The Pueblo Indians, like other primitive people, use masks in their ritual performances. These masks are made of wood, round, like inverted saucepans, and fit right over the head. The flattish top is decorated with feathers, and on the sides are wing-shaped ears.

Small models of these masked dancers are made as toys for the children, and the gifts are usually given at the conclusion of the festivals. The good Kachina carries dolls to the little Pueblo girls, and bows and arrows to the boys, in the manner of our own Father Christmas. It is a good way of introducing the religious beliefs to the children, and love and awe are inspired in their hearts. By this means they get used to the solemn rituals which are carried out at various seasons. Baby dolls also, fastened to cradle boards, are given to the small girls, complete with Kachina masks.

The country is searched far and wide for the cottonwood from which the masks and dolls are made. The men carve the wood with knives and rub it down with sandstone. The Hopi dolls are painted with brilliant colours, while those of the Zuñi Indians are usually white with splashes of bright colour. All manner of things go towards the decorating of these dolls, depending on which god they represent. Feathers, corn-husks, twigs, basketry and deerskin are fixed on and painted, and their clothes made of cotton cloth and woollen yarn.

The dolls represent almost every natural phenomenon, especially those connected with the weather. There are Kachinas for the seasons, rain, clouds, storms, and for birds, flowers, bees, snakes and things to do with the home and the hearth. They are complete little figures, rather square-looking, with sometimes a carved head under the mask which lifts off, or, again, just a mask alone, in which case it is carved in one with the body.

These Kachinas will be hung up on the whitewashed walls of the houses, together with rugs, herbals and calendars. Cottonwood prayer sticks hang from the rafters, and the Hopi people know that the dolls represent spiritual beings from the unseen world, and that their homes will be blessed and guarded. The religious rites are held in a 'Kiva', a kind of underground church, and although the Hopi people decorate their houses with the dolls, the Zuñi people will hide theirs away, and will not dream of selling them to sightseers.

Thousands of these dolls are made by the Hopi people, and visitors to these parts will see many for sale every year on stands by the roadside. These Kachinas will not have been used in religious rites, but will have been made especially to be sold as mementoes.

✳   ✳   ✳

The true folk doll in the U.S.A. is a rag doll, and these were made in the homes and dressed in bright cotton clothes. Corn-cobs, too, were used by early settlers when making dolls for their children, and these would be covered with pieces of cloth. Later, in the 17th and 18th centuries, in the New England homes, dolls were made in the shape of a cotton sack and stuffed and the faces indicated with ink or fruit juice, and yarn fixed to the tops of the dolls' heads to resemble hair. Rag dolls were made at home just as in England about the same period, some being made from patterns bought in shops.

A bride-doll is used at voodoo performances in New Orleans, together with blue candles and apples, and in California a grass doll is used by the Nischinham tribe for fertility reasons. Another curious item discovered in a search for dolls is a Kentucky superstition that a baby will die if it is carried in a funeral procession before it is a year old.

Dolls were listed as being a large article of manufacture in the *History of Manufactures in the U.S.A., 1860–1893*, and stuffed bodies for dolls were made in New York, Boston and Philadelphia, although the heads were mostly imported from abroad. There are so many dolls from this part of the world that more will be found about them later on under the heading of Dolls of Many Kinds.

Mary Ellen Chase mentions playing with dolls, in her book *The White Gate*, and Edna Woolman Chase gives an interesting piece about model dolls, in her book *Always in Vogue*, where she states that a Model Doll Show was held by *Vogue* for three years running, in 1896, 1897 and in 1898, this being an 'annual and charming event'.

New York. The dolls, miniature ladies in wax, about three and a half feet high, were beautifully modelled and dressed by the leading American designers. The first show was given for the benefit of the new Willard Parker Hospital, which was erected on the public land at Sixteenth Street near Avenue C, which has every advantage of isolation, and fronting on the broad East River receives pure fresh air from the water.

The affair went off in great style, for, according to the magazine's modest account of its own undertaking, 'it may be taken as an axiom that anything done by *Vogue*, or managed by it, will be well done. In evidence is the Model Doll Show that closed last Monday at Sharry's, a show that in variety, attractiveness and arrangements is second to nothing ever given in New York, and so extraordinarily successful as a first event that the augury for future years is most alluring.' The augury materialized for two years more, and then, for reasons to which I was not privy, abruptly ceased.

The idea of referring to dolls by their names seems to come from this country, and many dolls as soon as they are made are known as 'Alice' or 'Martha' or whatever name is chosen. In England a child may have a doll for a long time before giving it a name, and the firms do not name them as in the U.S.A., where we find such names as the Will Rogers doll, Annabel Lee dolls, Buster Brown and the Campbell Kids, and 'Poor Pitiful Pearl'. It is interesting that in the summer of 1959 'Pearl' was sent to Moscow to represent American dolls at the Exhibition of American products. Complete with a party frock she shows how a modern Cinderella can be transformed by a new dress and a 'pony-tail' hair-do.

There are wooden dolls carved in Tennessee, no two being made exactly alike. The first doll was named 'Holly' and after this all their dolls were known as 'Holly Dolls'.

Modern dolls are almost harking back to the fabulous ones of the 15th and 16th centuries in the matter of clothes. There are dolls with real silk stockings, nylon underwear and fur coats. In 1956, a maker of dolls in California claimed that he had sold 67 mink coats for dolls at the large sum of 295 dollars each!

The most sophisticated dolls in the whole world come from the United States. In the land where film-stars are born, dolls have a 'made-up' appearance, too-long eyelashes, dyed and waved hair and red finger and toe nails. Some have shapely figures, in fact many have returned to the 'grown-up' age of the period before dolls were made as children. They are very expensive and wear costly clothes, including mink stoles, nylon stockings, lace underwear and high-heeled shoes. In the *New York Times*, December 1957, a mother writes objecting to these shapely dolls; 'I object strenuously to awakening sexual curiosity in little ones at such a tender age, via dolls sporting a tantalizing peekaboo negligé'.

There are baby dolls as well as the grown-up kind, these being almost too natural. Not only can they feed from small bottles, but they wear nappies, i.e. diapers, which they can use also! A young American girl told me that this gives a lot of work in the matter of drying, and probably many children prefer a cuddly rag doll to one of these, which leaves nothing to the imagination.

Dolls' kitchens, also, are fitted with all the latest gadgets, modern equipment including washing machines, food-mixers, refrigerators and whistling kettles, all of which are worked by electric batteries. This gives some idea of the background against which a modern doll might live.

'Poor Pitiful Pearl'
A doll which can be undressed, bathed and have her Saran hair arranged in different ways. 18-in. high. 1959
A Glad Toy weighing 27 ozs. U.S.A. Lent by Mrs Graham Greene

Prehistoric pottery doll, about 6 in. high. California
Doll with movable joints. Teotihuacan, Mexico
Small clay figure, 8 in. high, A.D. 100–200, found buried in Mexico

See opposite page

Stuffed buckskin doll, dressed in buckskin, 14 in. high. Horniman Museum, London, England

Doll in buckskin clothes with real hair, probably 19th century, 8 in. high. Horniman Museum

Eskimo man doll carrying a large red bow. Made of buckskin and beads and with real hair. 9 in. high. Pitt Rivers Museum, Oxford

Eskimo woman doll, made in the same manner, dressed in buckskin, trimmed with beads, features worked in coloured beads. Horniman Museum

Tall Eskimo man doll, kid limbs, wooden face, dressed completely in furs. 10 in. high. Labrador
Pitt Rivers Museum, Oxford

Boy Eskimo doll, dressed in English-made flannel, wearing tiny gloves and boots.
The flannel will have been brought in a whaling ship

Eskimo doll dressed in furs

Eskimo doll of carved ivory, 3 in. high. Imperial Institute, London

Canadian doll of buckskin, bead features, buckskin clothes. 10 in. high
National Museum of Canada, Ottawa, Ontario

1. Charm for a boy in the form of a rattle-snake, procured from 'Eagle Speaker', a Blood Indian. 10 in. high, elliptical in section.   2. Charm for a girl, procured from a Blood Indian called 'Standing Alone', 6in. high, elliptical section. Horniman Museum.   3. Doll in a leather carrier embroidered with beads. From the Flat-head tribe, people who make baskets and love children.   4. Papoose in a baby-carrier. A characteristic toy of a little American Indian girl. North-west coast. Collected in the U.S.A. by Sir Henry Wellcome. Wellcome Museum, London. 5. Modern baby doll from Canada. Plastic face, painted features, black hair, plastic headband and feather. There is no body, just stuffing; the whole doll resting on a cardboard carrier, 4 in. long. Lent by Mrs Harrison

American Indian man doll, carved from a wooden base and covered with felt. Dressed in a blanket with folded arms fixed to body. The rough body is of coarse muslin, stuffed with straw, wooden legs coated with skin. Arms, pads beneath the dyed, patterned blanket, the face is a mask with no neck. 10½ in. high. Horniman Museum
American Indian Squaw doll, carrying a baby. Made in the same way as the man, but with cotton dress peeping beneath her blanket. They both wear leather shoes, and the baby has a leather circlet on its head. The baby is simply padding with a mask added. Their garments do not come off. Horniman Museum, London

Seminole dolls made of palmetto fibre, dressed in long bands of coloured material stitched together by machine

1

Doll from the South Western States, dressed in a white, navy
and red robe with a head-dress decorated with feathers, a
Kachina doll wearing a mask. British Museum, London

2

Baby doll on a cradle board and wearing a Kachina mask. Figurines of this kind were given to little girls at festivals.
This one has a greenish mask, red ears and features, black eyes and reddish cloth feet. Cradle board dull red colour
with leather thongs. Wellcome Museum

1. Pueblo doll, 4½ in. high. British Museum

2. Doll of the Tewa Indians, wearing a feather on its hea

Kachina dolls given to Pueblo boys and girls

in. high. Arizona. Pitt Rivers Museum, Oxford

3. Pueblo doll with feather head-dress. 8½ in. high
British Museum

All of these dolls are very light to hold

3

25

Doll from New Mexico of orange-tinted leather with horsehair for hair. Bead features. 12 in. high
Pitt Rivers Museum, Oxford
Clown from the Tewa Indians, Arizona. Pinkish clay with painted bands of pink and black. Very heavy to hold, and may be a fertility figure. 10 in. high. Pitt Rivers Museum, Oxford

AMERICAN NEGRESS DOLL, about 1865.

2nd petticoat of fawn muslin, with slight rib.

stitched here to the hem.

1st petticoat, white, glazed and starched.

Black leather, piped with blue ribbon, brown sole, blue bow and silver buckle.

Deep hem.

Dress of glazed chintz with self white pattern.

Very long white cotton socks, one with inital G at the side

Black silk apron, with two black bands of velvet. Red chain stitch on collar and cuffs. Cotton hanky on head.
Black leather hands.
Black fabric body, stuffed with sawdust.
Total height, 16 inches.

Details of doll on following page

27

American Negress doll of stuffed black fabric with black leather hands, dressed in a chintz gown and black apron. 1865. 16 in. high. Given by the Baroness Roeder to Bethnal Green Museum, London

Modern American doll given me by Mrs Beulah Hawkins of California. Movable eyes, head and arms joined by a continuous piece of elastic. 8 in. high

Ideal doll, U.S.A. One of the rubber baby dolls which were some of the last to arrive in England from America just before the 1939 war. Lent by Mrs Gordon Coles

Four fertility figures, about 1000 B.C. Mexico

The people of Mexico have had dolls for a very long time, and small ones have been found attributed to the 10th and 11th centuries A.D. These are made of clay with movable arms and legs, with holes in the bodies through which strings were passed in the same manner as those of the Greeks and the Romans. The early Mexican toy animals also resemble those of the Greeks, with their wheels made from tubes of clay and possibly with wooden axles.

A few small figures were found buried during the excavations at Teotihuacan, but what they were for, no one knows. Attributed to the Toltec people, they had human faces modelled true to life, and may have been portraits of different racial types. They were made of clay and are about $1\frac{1}{2}$ inches high.

The famous Aztec ruler, Montezuma, was also said to have played with dolls.

Heads of dolls, from the valley of Mexico, made of fawn, pinkish baked clay, and built up of round sausage-like lumps, with deep eyes in deep sockets. About the time of Christ. Camborne Museum, Cornwall

Doll from Guatemala. Handmade over a wire frame covered with thin brown paper. Face of woven cloth and wool features. Hat of straw and string, coarse woven apron and cotton trousers. A rush mat on his back. 7 in. high
Lent by Miss Juliet Russell

The Pipil dolls from El Salvador, in Central America, have the upper parts of their faces painted pink and white. The lower parts of the cheek and jaw are painted a dark blue to indicate beards and they have black painted moustaches. The faces are flat and the eyes blue with long dark eyelashes.

Some of the dolls in Panama wear skirts made of grass or from palm leaves, and near the lower reaches of the Rio Pirri, where the native women paint their faces with red lines, the same colouring is copied on the dolls. The women wear coloured skirts, and the men have long hair, metal rings around their wrists and also red and white faces. Some even gild their teeth and paint themselves with black pitch, so there seems to be no end to how a doll might appear in order to be in the fashion of the time.

Gentleman and lady dolls from Costa Rica.
Beautifully made from palm leaves.
Grassy brown hair. 12 in. high
Pitt Rivers Museum, Oxford

Doll from Central America,
carrying a baby, and both with
pink-striped faces. 6 in. high.
Pitt Rivers Museum, Oxford

Doll from ancient Peru made of coarse woven canvas and stuffed. Dressed in finely woven canvas, tied with string.
At the hem is a beautifully woven design of cats and flying birds. The cat form or panther frequently appears
on these Peruvian materials. 16 in. high. British Museum

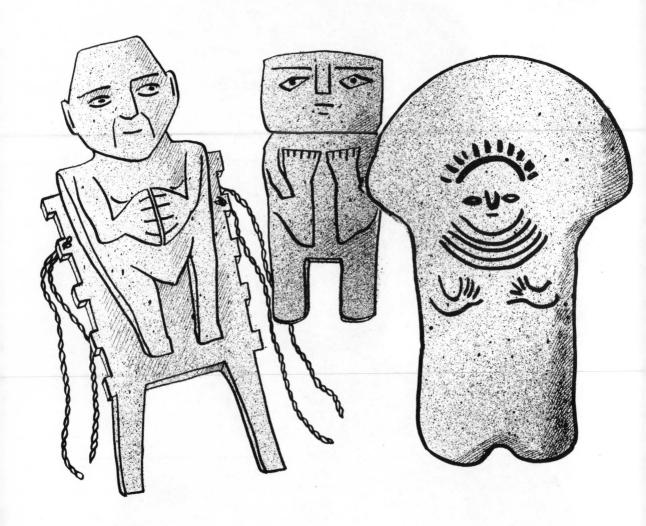

Wooden baby doll on a cradle board, like a butcher's tray. Cords or leather thongs to tie the baby in. Peru

Flat, carved baby doll made in one with the tray. The legs are in a tucked-up position

Ancient clay doll from Peru, of a dull pinkish colour. 6 in. high. Pitt Rivers Museum, Oxford

Ancient clay doll wearing a hat with a feather. Peru

Ancient Peruvian doll with features and hands indicated in paint. Found buried in a child's grave in the cemetery at Ancon

Clay doll from Ancon

Woven dolls from ancient Peru, one holding a spinning whorl. One doll is of twisted cane, covered with cloth and string, and wrapped in woven material, the other is bound round with string and dressed in woven cloth
8 in. high. British Museum

Ancient Peruvian dolls of pottery. Each has a hole on either side. The reddish one is from Chancay. British Museum

Eye ○○○○ White
     ○○○○ Blue
     ○○○○ White

Doll from Peru made of coarse fawn canvas, blue and white bead features, real black hair. Wears a navy blue robe
trimmed with white beads arranged in pairs. 13¾ in. high. Bethnal Green Museum

Wooden doll from ancient Peru, very dark with a flat back, metal eyes and teeth. 5 in. high. British Museum

Tall wooden doll from Jauja, Peru. Brownish colour, one of the few wooden dolls from South America.
Pitt Rivers Museum, Oxford

Dolls from the Indians of the Chaco, showing tattoo marks representing various things. Amongst these there are three tall thin men and two women carrying babies.

Two Choroti dolls on donkeys, need great imagination, as all breakable parts have been left off beforehand

Aymara doll. An Indian masked dancer, leather sandals and hands. Doll of stuffed cloth, flat leather hands. Mask pulls over the face like a hood, fastened at the back where it comes to a point. 8 in. high, head-dress 2½ in. higher. 1895. La Paz, Bolivia. Given by Miss C. M. Mugford to Bethnal Green Museum

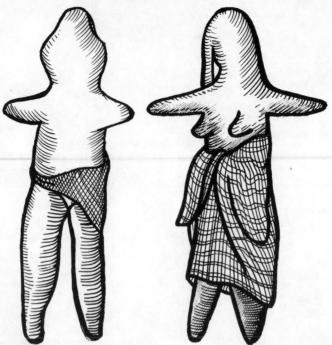

Male and female wax dolls from the Indians of the Chaco, draped in cloth. Chanés du Rio Parapîte

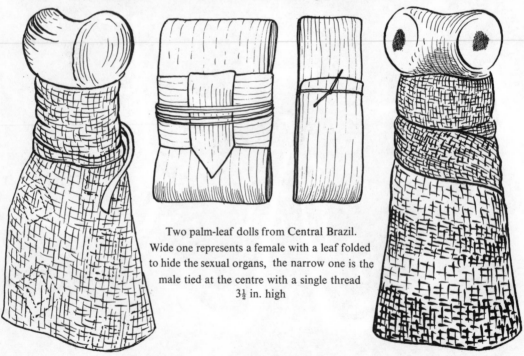

Two palm-leaf dolls from Central Brazil.
Wide one represents a female with a leaf folded
to hide the sexual organs, the narrow one is the
male tied at the centre with a single thread
$3\frac{1}{2}$ in. high

Two Lenguan dolls made from ostrich bones and dressed in cloth

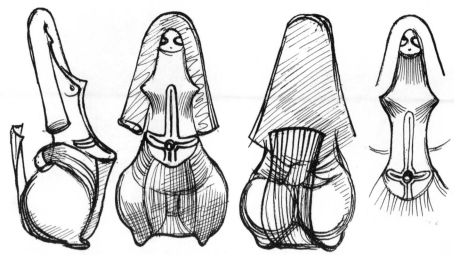

A curious doll from Brazil, probably connected with fertility. Made of greyish coloured clay, with black markings, with raffia coloured skirt made to flap back. Quite heavy to hold. 4 in. high. British Museum

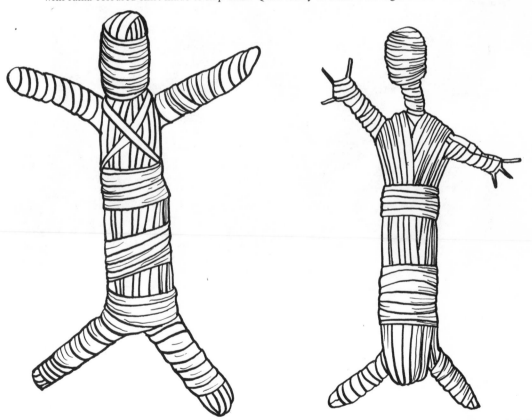

Two straw dolls from Central Brazil. Used to indicate a festival in a nearby house where they are displayed. Jolly dolls, known as 'an invitation to the dance', they have nothing sinister about them. 8 in. high

Fruit vendor from Brazil carrying a piccaninny on her back. Made of stuffed black poplin, with two stiff buckram petticoats under her dress. Poplin hands carefully made. 1890. 11 in. high. Given by Miss E. J. White to the Bethnal Green Museum

Modern Brazilian doll, made over a wire frame with material and stuffing, painted features, a much-padded bosom, thin wrists, broad legs, flat felt feet strengthened with cardboard so that she can stand. Stitched clothes, apron edged with cotton braid and tied. Felt bodice pointed at the back where the straps meet. Cotton blouse, petticoat, pants, woven skirt, felt hem, wool embroidery and sequins. Brass earrings and beads

Lent by Miss Juliet Russell

45

Doll from Uruguay dressed as a fruit vendor, made like the doll from Brazil. 11 in. high

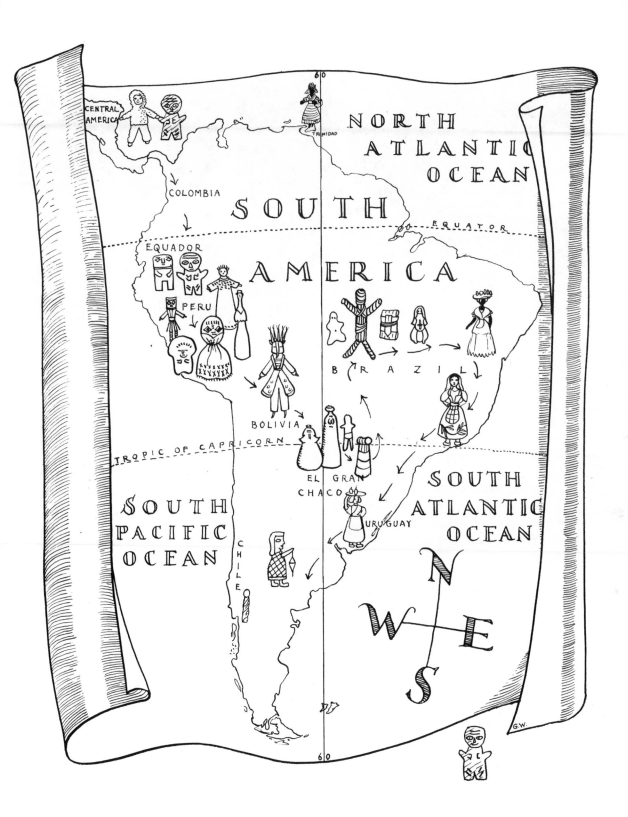

Woven motifs of cats

DOLLS OF SOUTH AMERICA

In Colombia there are rattle dolls made of clay, in Ecuador are dolls carved from the ivory nut palm, in Peru are beautifully made woven dolls and in the Chaco territories are some extraordinary little dolls of clay. There are not many carved wooden dolls, but the native women of Peru sometimes carry a wooden doll on their backs to represent a lost infant.

Ancon, in Peru, was an ancient burying place and many playthings have come to light during excavations from time to time. Among these are dolls, dolls' clothes and little utensils, all of which have been buried along with their owners. The dry earth of these parts has helped to preserve them and some dolls found have even been prepared as mummies and swathed in cotton in the same way as the bodies of the children.

There are clay dolls pressed in moulds and strongly made, with large heads and small arms. Some dolls have painted faces and others were made from various materials such as fibre or crudely plaited straw, and a very few from carved wood. The dolls were intended to be dressed in cloth and some were ornamented with shells and feathers.

In the Inca cities of Peru there were dolls made of brass, stone and tapestry. The latter are true rag dolls, unbreakable, and many of these have survived, although the woven features gradually disappear. More recent than the tapestry dolls are ones dressed in striped cotton, made up of a single strip, folded in half, longways on, and then sewn up as far as the arm openings.

Baby dolls dressed in swaddling clothes are very interesting, particularly as baby dolls were not made in Europe until the middle of the 19th century. Some baby dolls are fixed to cradle boards, and others like this have been found in Mexico.

Frequently in the woven dresses of the dolls occurs the picture of a cat, which has a religious significance. Sometimes it is just the head of a smiling cat, sometimes the whole body, and even an embroidered cat with another cat inside it, and yet another cat inside that, reminding one of a Russian nest doll, and all fitting one inside the other.

Bone dolls are made in the Rio Negro district, with mother-of-pearl eyes, and other dolls are of plaited bark decorated with feathers. The Katiueo tribe carves dolls from wood and in Bolivia there are primitive specimens of wax, some of which are dressed in cloth. Others made of resin are dressed in paper.

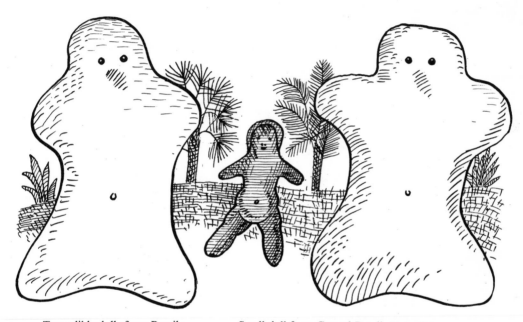

Two edible dolls from Brazil   Small doll from Central Brazil. Not edible

In Brazil there are dolls made of clay and the clay dolls of the Bakari in Central Brazil are made from loam which is heavy and of a reddish colour. This loam is a kind of edible clay which the children are fond of licking and sometimes while they are standing around talking, bits of the loam will be picked off the clay houses and eaten. Their forefathers ate it and it almost looks like a kind of fat heavy dough.

There is a harder kind of clay from which dolls are also made, but this is not edible, and they are played with by the older children. These are small, about $3\frac{1}{2}$ inches high, whereas the edible ones are bigger, being about 6 to 9 inches high, and except for currants they are much the same shape as the European ones of dough.

In some parts of Brazil the native women paint their babies red, and hang necklaces of seeds and teeth round their necks.

In Paraguay are some roughly carved wooden dolls, usually made by the boys.

✳   ✳   ✳

The flat inland plain bordering Argentina, Bolivia and Paraguay is known as the Chaco. It is inhabited by twelve Indian tribes. The Lenguan Indians live in the Paraguayan Chaco – the name Gran Chaco meaning the Great Hunt.

The religion of the Lenguans forbids them to mention the name of a dead Lenguan or anything about him, and as all his possessions are destroyed, it is difficult to picture what the children's toys were like or how they spent their leisure.

They are fond of children but they have a dread of evil spirits. The women spin and weave clothes for their menfolk, but wear skirts of skins themselves and they carry the children about and also the luggage. This is in order that the men are left free to chase and shoot the wild animals, and even the little boys of three years old can shoot with bows and arrows at quickly darting lizards.

The Lenguans make musical instruments from wood and carved gourds, and even the women and the children smoke. While their mothers are weaving, the girls watch and also play at making pots and toy clay animals which are hardened in hot ashes.

Their dolls are made from the knuckle-bones of ostriches, and the young children play with string and make cats' cradles.

The children wear necklaces of beads, shells and sheep's teeth and put feathers in their hair, and around their ankles they put more feathers to protect them from snakebite. They wear rugs round their shoulders in cold weather and round their waists in hot weather, and their blankets are of many colours and patterns, the red dye coming from a tree. They have browny red skins, black eyes and long black hair and they wrap up their dolls in the same way as themselves.

✳   ✳   ✳

Among the Chaco Indians are some most interesting clay dolls made by the Choroti women. While they are making their pottery vessels, with their small daughters watching, they will take a lump of clay and fashion it into a doll.

These dolls almost resemble tumbler dolls, as the base is rounded and they have neither arms nor legs. The boy dolls are shaped rather like ninepins and the females are rounder and fatter and always with protruding breasts. Sometimes the female dolls carry babies and these will have a rug indicated in the form of a sling, but never any limbs, the reason being that they crack off so easily.

When a mother doll is holding a baby doll, extreme care is taken to model the breasts in a downward direction in readiness for a feed, and these are the only dolls in which this detail occurs.

The dolls are not large, being about 2¼ to 3 inches high, though some are bigger and a few of the boy dolls are as much as 8 inches high. The toy mules on which they sit are about 3 inches across.

Some may be strengthened inside with grass, otherwise no foreign element is added. No wood-carving tools, no iron knife, not even a pencil goes towards the carving of the clay dolls, which are modelled with the hands alone and perhaps the detail added with the help of a stiff blade of grass for marking. The limbs are omitted because they break off too soon, as the toys are not baked but are merely left to dry in the sun or very slowly in front of a fire.

The most important thing about these dolls is their tattoo marks. These are faithfully copied from those made on the faces of the children, which indicate their various ages.

A different design is used denoting the age of the child, whether it is a boy or a girl, and in the case of a girl the tattoo marks will indicate when she is ready for marriage. These marks are copied on the dolls depending to which child they belong, and both girls and boys have long black hair. The red colour used on the faces of the children and on the doll is extracted from the seeds of a local bush, and the yellow comes from a root, but the black is simply soot mixed with spit. All these tattoo marks are painted on the bodies of the dolls as there is no room for them on their little button heads, and the female dolls are stouter to enable the marks to be indicated in their entirety.

In the case of the female dolls, the eyes are painted on the breasts, the nose marks in between and the hair is suggested by ridge marks down either side and on the back of the lumpy body.

These dolls are definitely playthings and have no other significance, and the children get much delight from using their imagination. They sit the dolls on mules which look almost like mushrooms and indeed a stranger would hardly suppose that the lumps of clay represented both girl and boy dolls, and that the little 'stools' were wagons.

The dolls have no value as a means of exchange, but when dolls are made representing white people, they are more realistic with the addition of arms and legs.

✳ ✳ ✳

Drawing to show how the tattoo marks on a girl's face are copied onto the body of a girl doll, and similarly with that belonging to a boy. Choroti people

Corn bird, known as a Harpi scarer,
used to scare away evil spirits

Straw dolls, very much like the ones found in Europe, are also made in parts of South America, but these are merry, jolly dolls and have no sinister meaning.

These straw dolls are made with the arms and legs stretched out; sometimes the toes and the fingers are indicated. Some are playthings for children, others are used as signs and will be put on the roof of a hut during festival time. Their presence shows that the festivities will take place in that hut and by this means the doll communicates the news to the surrounding people. In 1884 these straw figures were fairly large, but now they are smaller and often are carried around on the head for the same purpose and indicate an 'invitation to the dance'.

Mostly built up of straw, these dolls are hollow in the centre, and have leaves and foliage and, in some, a button on the top for a head.

Straw birds, also, are put on the roofs of the houses, but these are 'Harpi destructors' and are for frightening away the Monsters of South America, which include eagles, the birds of prey. Made from maize cobs and straw, they are decorated with coloured ribbons and often have real feathers in the tails which are painted with black stripes. The toes are carefully finished at the ends, with twisted straw, in the same manner as the dolls.

Palm leaves form another kind of doll, and these are carefully made by the children. A doll, to represent a girl, will have a leaf folded over in order to hide her private parts, and a boy doll will be longer and thinner, with his 'middle' tied by a single thread. These dolls are quite small, being about 3 inches high when folded, whereas the straw dolls mentioned above are about 9 inches long.

Among the Aymara Indians, masks are worn at their ritual dances, and dolls representing these dancers are made wearing complete masks over the heads.

In the Argentine, dolls are made from rhea bones, a rhea being a small three-toed ostrich. I do not know whether there is any connection between a rhea bone doll, and Rhea, the mother of the Gods in Greece. The female dolls are dressed in petticoats and the male ones are wrapped in rugs.

✳   ✳   ✳

In southern Chile, dolls are made to lie in babies' cradles as the real babies do, and these cradles are rather like the old-fashioned trays used by butchers' boys. Some are of wood, while others may be of plaited straw, with a loop at one end. The children prop these up against the walls of their rooms, just as their mothers do with the real babies. This seems a good idea, as the baby can watch what is going on.

✳   ✳   ✳

Some of the best modern dolls of South America are made in Bolivia and Chile. Made on a wire frame and covered with woollen knitting and crochet, they have real hair added and ornaments of glass beads. In the large towns, there will be modern dolls like the ones from Europe and the U.S.A., and many of them have a definite Spanish look about them, with their swirling skirts, dark hair and dark eyes. Brown-eyed dolls have always sold better in these countries than blue-eyed ones, but in England blue-eyed dolls have been popular since the reign of Queen Victoria.

Doll from Trinidad. lent by Miss Marjorie Lander

53

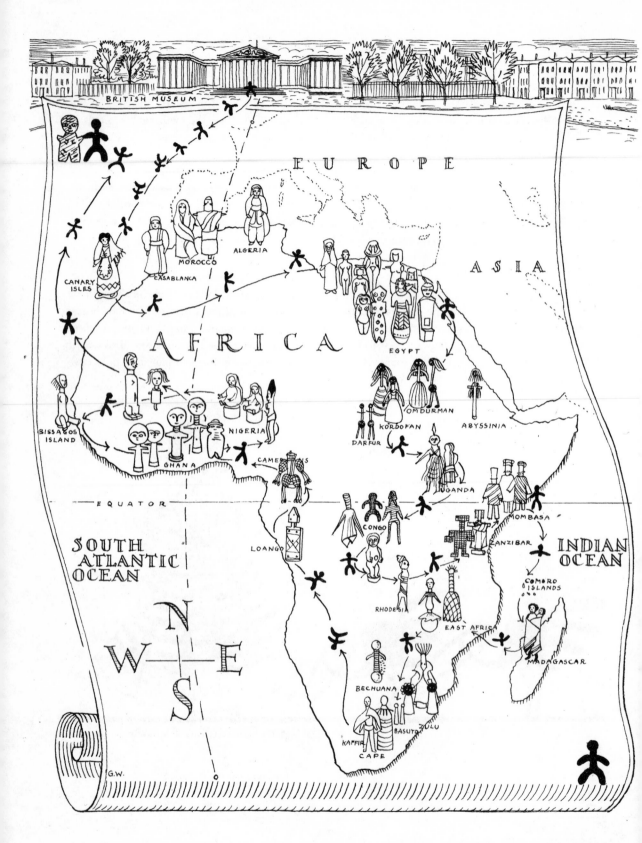

BRITISH MUSEUM

EUROPE

ASIA

AFRICA

CANARY ISLES

MOROCCO

CASABLANCA

ALGERIA

EGYPT

OMDURMAN

ABYSSINIA

BISSAGOS ISLAND

NIGERIA

DARFUR

KORDOFAN

GHANA

CAMEROONS

UGANDA

EQUATOR

LOANGO

CONGO

MOMBASA

SOUTH ATLANTIC OCEAN

ZANZIBAR

INDIAN OCEAN

COMORO ISLANDS

RHODESIA

EAST AFRICA

MADAGASCAR

N W E S

BECHUANA

KAFFIR

CAPE

BASUTO

ZULU

G.W.

DOLLS OF AFRICA

A varied array of dolls comes from Africa. Some are playthings, others are made for fertility reasons and many have their shape and features, or rather the lack of them, influenced by religion.

On the north coast there are dolls imported from Europe and these may be clothed by natives in their own costume. A Moorish girl, given a European doll, will undress it and clothe it again in simple desert style. Among the Tuaregs, the men wear veils, and not the women, and the dolls do likewise.

Many native girls are married before fifteen years old, but they still play with dolls, and there are dolls for children, dolls for when a woman wishes to have a child and dolls used by medicine-men and in native dances.

The headless dolls, and those without features, which from time to time have been unearthed from graves, belonged to Jewish children or to Egyptian children who had been converted to the Hebrew faith. The Mosaic law forbade the reproduction of the human face and ancient Jewish dolls throughout the world have no features. In the same way, Mohammed declared that 'Every representation of this kind would be placed before its author on the Judgement Day, and he would be commanded to put life into it, which not being able to do, he would be cast for a time into Hell.' Some Moslems believe that sculptures casting shadows are unlawful, which would not include flat representations.

It must not be assumed that all small figures discovered during excavations are dolls, because this would be far from the truth. Often they were made especially for putting in temples or to be carried at fêtes. Nevertheless, these little things might find their way into the hands of children, and providing they were not endowed with evil powers, they might become playthings.

The dolls of Egypt are well known, especially the flat ones of wood, with gaily painted patterns. Here again, these dolls are so old that their true purpose has been lost, but whatever it was, surely they ended up in a baby's hands and their bead hair was made to jump about and rattle.

The flat spade-like body of these dolls looks almost as if it had been cut with a fretsaw from wood about one-eighth of an inch thick, the head often left flat, but sometimes having a protruding face of clay. The body is decorated with typical Egyptian ornament and the squares and triangles coloured with earthy colours, ochre, red and black. The 'hair' is made up of small grey beads of mud from the bank of the Nile, which is rolled and threaded and often finished off with a brighter bead at the tip or an elongated grey one.

Other dolls have movable limbs worked with strings, and were in use before the towns of Athens and Rome were begun. Some of the limbs of these dolls were attached with pins, the marks clearly showing, and other rigid dolls were made from bronze, limestone, earthenware and porcelain. There were beautiful, smooth dolls of blue-glazed porcelain also, but these must have been easily breakable and not so strong as the ones of wood.

Dolls buried in the graves of the ancient Egyptians were known as 'ushabti' or answerers, rendering service to the one with whom they were buried and some even had a bellows-like instrument inside. It was also the custom to bury a child's playthings with it and in this case the little figures would be genuine dolls, with miniature objects for the 'dolls' houses'. Many of these have been found in the regions around Thebes, on the banks of the Nile, known as the Valley of the Kings and now partially occupied by the towns of Luxor and Karnak.

A few dolls found in graves are said to be the figures of concubines, with legs joined together, to prevent them from running away. As early as 2000 B.C. there were clapper dolls in Egypt, some very carefully carved. Other dolls were used as substitutes for children, as offerings to the River Nile when the waters did not rise at the proper time. Instead of a child being thrown in the waters, a doll was used instead, and often these were made of straw or of reeds, not carefully made, as they soon sank in the water.

The little Roman rag-doll found at Oxyrrhynchus in Egypt is made of coarse woven material, and may have had two blue beads for eyes and a face indicated by stitches. Other dolls belonging to the 6th and 7th centuries A.D. have been clothed in woollen dresses.

✳   ✳   ✳

In the Sudan there are curious dolls which are connected with witchcraft and magic. The childless women purchase these from old 'witches' in order that they may have children, and having bought them at quite a high price they carry the doll around on their backs. Should they get a child of their own later on, the doll will be highly prized, but if not, the doll will be discarded and sold off at a reduced price.

These dolls are characteristic, with very long necks, topped with a lump of clay for a head, another clay lump for a body and two long legs about the same length as the neck and as thick. Sometimes the body is of twisted cane, but the feet are just two lumps of clay, and the arms hang limply down, being made of material and stuffed like sausages and the ends rounded and tied, with no attempt at hands. The large eyes are of pearl, the poorer variety having buttons instead, but all the faces have two green marks on each cheek and a wonderful head of 'hair' made from coarse black wool, each strand having a lump of grey clay at the extreme end.

The important thing about these dolls is their jewellery. They are loaded down with ornaments, charms and amulets, with necklaces hanging down to their waists and with bracelets around their wrists. The more ornaments the more expensive will the doll be to purchase. They manage to achieve quite an air of distinction, with their cotton skirts gathered at the waist and reaching to the feet, in spite of their crude shape, and by the time they are loaded with 'jewels' they are fairly heavy to hold. The height of these dolls varies between 10 and 15 inches.

✳   ✳   ✳

Some of the most primitive dolls of all are found in Central Africa, many being mere lumps of wood. Indeed, too lifelike a doll might be considered as uncanny, and a parent, thinking it might do the child harm, will make money by selling it as a fetish.

Among the people of the Achewa tribe, spirit dolls are made from pieces of wood about 2 or 3 inches long. These pieces are bound together with strips of fabric or bark rope, to resemble the figure of a doll.

Three dolls from the Sudan, made of cane and clay, and with stuffed arms. Pitt Rivers Museum, Oxford

They believe that the spirits of their dead will enter the bodies of the dolls.

Other tribes will conceal a box, made from a gourd and shaped like an old-fashioned pillbox, inside the doll and wrapping the whole thing around with cloth, they believe that the spirit of their ancestor is captured within the box.

Around the village of Mkoma, dolls are treasured as household gods, and sacrifices and prayers are offered to them. The spirits are objects of worship among the Achewa people and the Bantu tribes.

Three spirit dolls from the Congo, one of a dead chief from Central Africa, one of iron with holes for eyes

The iron dolls from the Congo must surely be the most unbreakable in the whole world, but often they belong to the chiefs and are not playthings. They have arms and legs and sometimes the head is hollow. They also have spirit dolls, in which the spirit of the dead is captured without the need of a box, as in parts of China.

The village doctor will cure tummy-ache by means of a doll. This doll is made of wood and has a carved hole in the front into which he will put medicine. As the doll is placed in an appointed place away from the house, he may never even see the patient with the stomach pains.

In parts of the Congo, little playthings have been found on children's graves, such as dolls' heads, toy animals, miniature pitchers and wash bowls.

Girls are trained to carry babies on their backs by carrying pineapples, and in the Congo, the little cannibals will imitate their parents by tying dolls to their backs. These are made from cassava roots or pieces of stick and wrapped around with rags. As flour is made from these roots the cassava dolls are edible, which is rather interesting, considering that these children are cannibals.

The Pygmy children play at cat's cradles, using their feet as well as their hands. It is a common sight to see a small girl staggering under the weight of her baby brother, so perhaps there is not much time for them to play with dolls; in any case I have not discovered any from amongst the Pygmy people. A Bambuti child wears nothing in the way of clothes, but when a boy reaches four years old, he wears a loincloth.

The Ovampo people have dolls called children and these are most carefully guarded. If a hut should catch fire, the first thing to rescue is the girl's doll, for among many of the African people the belief exists that harm will come to the owner of the doll and the original owner if it has been handed on, and consequently dolls are rather difficult to obtain. When the owner of a doll is promised in marriage, the future husband will give the doll a name and this same name is given to the first child of the marriage. The eldest daughter inherits her mother's doll.

✳   ✳   ✳

Amongst the Ila-speaking people of Northern Rhodesia are dolls made from Munkulungu wood, which are ornamented with strings of beads. These wooden dolls are called 'mwana wa chrisamo' and are used in initiation ceremonies. The drawing shows a Ba-ila doll, Ba being the word for doll. Made of dark brown wood, it has beads for hair and is not a plaything. However, in their play, the girls use dolls almost exclusively and these they make from corn-cobs or mealie-cobs as they are known. With them they play at families and build miniature villages. The maize corn-cob does not look much like a doll, but the top-knot of 'hair' is carefully arranged, and these girls derive their enjoyment from arranging the hair in the latest style of that part of the country; sometimes parting it in the centre and sometimes at the side, they spend hours playing with these corn-cobs.

In the swampy regions of the White Nile, the children play at weddings, although most little Africans are kept busy doing chores. The boys make clay figures and colour them with ash or charred wood and if they make a drawing of a human figure, it is usually rectangular in shape.

In other parts of Kenya, girls carry dolls on their backs and women carry them for fertility reasons, these dolls being usually made from gourds. On the island of Comoro, where many of the inhabitants are Moslems, their religion forbids the making of a human face, so the dolls here are the featureless kind. Zanzibar, too, has this kind of doll and also dolls made from the local palm-leaves. The leaves are threaded and plaited for the dolls, and the arms and legs are made of threaded nuts, the dolls being fairly strong as the leaves dry and stiffen.

✳   ✳   ✳

In Somaliland there are dolls made from bones and these have bead features and black woolly hair. Beads are universally prized among all African tribes and they form a ready and convenient item as a means of exchange. Quantities of these are imported from Birmingham, especially the brightly coloured small variety, but the better quality ones are made in Paris and Venice. Many antique beads were found in the Egyptian tombs.

Kaffir dolls are often made of strong, reddish-coloured leather, and stuffed, and others are made from clay and baked in the sun. There are also dolls made from corn-cobs, with bead eyes and hair of blanket thread. Many of the dolls in South Africa are dressed entirely in beads over a wooden foundation and others are of stuffed material with bead eyes.

The dolls of the Basuto people are especially jolly, with round faces of black cotton material, bead eyes and black woolly hair. Large beads of a grey colour sometimes do for 'hair', similar in colour to those used on the Egyptian dolls. The wooden or stuffed bodies are wound around with threaded beads which often make beautiful patterns, and as these dolls have no legs, they stand firmly on the ground like the well-known nest dolls of Russia. Basuto women desiring children carry on their backs very heavy dolls, known as Suchasis.

When a girl in the Fingo reaches marriageable age she is given a doll which she keeps until she has a child of her own. When she does, her mother gives her another doll until the girl has a second child, and this goes on until she has quite a family of dolls as well as children. The dolls are treated with care and arranged on stools in the house.

* * *

Amongst the Fali tribe in the French Cameroons, dolls play an important part as gifts or tokens of friendship. They are exchanged when the friendship is sealed and are offered to the best friends, with the saying 'I give you my head'. The dolls are carefully kept to preserve the friendship. A boy gives one doll to his favourite girl, and she will carry it pick-a-back fashion, or prop it against the wall of her home. If the girl marries the boy-friend, she keeps the doll until the birth of her first child, and when her last child is born, the doll is kept in a corner of the room and takes no further part in the activities of the household.

These dolls are made from corn-cobs or of wood. The wooden kind is made from a stick of wood which has been stripped of the bark and polished. A lump of wax forms the head; human hair is sunk into this and arranged with beads, some being coated with red colouring matter.

Other dolls may have arms and legs of leather, the ends being cut into thongs, on which are threaded cowrie shells and beads to represent fingers and toes, five on each. These dolls are dressed as natives, sometimes with cotton trousers or merely a single strip folded round the body. They are adorned with jewels, elaborate bead collars and perhaps more cowrie shells. Animal or human hair is put on the heads, and this is decorated with beads or pierced iron rings.

Sometimes a doll will be made representing a dead child and will be kept as a memorial to it. Wax babies have often been made for this purpose in parts of Europe also.

* * *

The Bechuanas carry a doll with them when the women marry and they keep this until they have a child of their own. These dolls simply consist of a long calabash, resembling a bottle, and this is wound round and round with strings of beads. The Basuto women do the same thing, but theirs are often made of clay and these will be treated like children and given names.

Dolls are used in various ceremonies in West Africa. Apart from being playthings, they will be used as tokens of love and affection and also as signs for when a child is ill.

A mother with a sick child will place one of these dolls in a spot indicated by the medicine-man. This is usually near her home and she also puts a gift beside it. Many of these dolls used for 'magical' purposes have a resinous sticky excretion applied to their faces, and a whitish substance is also smeared on the dolls which are used in fertility rites.

Wooden doll from Central Africa. Modern

Doll. Suchasis. Carried on the back of a Basuto woman who wishes to have offspring. Horniman Museum

Large dolls are carried on the backs of women in Senegal and on the Ivory Coast. These indicate that the girls are ready for marriage, or that the women desire children. Made of wood, these dolls are carried across the back much in the same manner as the forked sticks are carried in Australia.

In Nigeria there are dolls made of wax and these are found also among the Hausa tribe, but mostly in this region the dolls are made of wood.

Three Ashanti dolls of dark wood and wearing beads. 13 in. high. Wellcome Museum, London

The flat wooden dolls along this coast are a light colour when new, but they gradually become dark with age. These dolls are spoon-shape, with carved features, and their bodies are almost like stands. The Ashanti dolls are called 'Akua mma', and are carved to represent the local idea of beauty, and these are carried by young girls in order that they may grow up attractive. Some have bead hair, but they are mostly left plain, or they may have holes pierced at the sides to take earrings. The long necks of the dolls are either smoothly finished, or they may be carved with rings. As dolls, they are nice and smooth to hold and can be laid flat on the ground at night-time.

Pregnant women also carry the black Ashanti dolls, hoping that the long-shaped necks and beautiful heads will help them to bear children like them. During this time they are careful not to look at anything which is ugly, and not even at a monkey, for fear they should bear a child like it.

Three new dolls from Ashanti. Pale colour smooth wood, rounded bodies, and flat heads. 9 in. high
Imperial Institute, London

On the coast, figures may be made at the time of a man's death and although the Atutu people are not ancestor worshippers, they believe that the soul of the dead man will enter this figure for a while before passing into the beyond. Sometimes, if someone is in trouble, the village magician will advise him to have a fetish made and this will be made by a wood-carver and sprinkled with a white chalky substance or even with flour. These fetishes will be kept if the desired result is obtained, otherwise they will be thrown away.

Women desiring children will sometimes have dolls made from gourds, though the wooden kind are more usual. The doll will be thrown away if no child arrives, or given away as a plaything, but should the woman get a child, then the doll is considered valuable and may be used again and again, and carried on her back. The Atutu children as well as the adults have carefully carved dolls made especially as playthings, having no magical or religious significance whatever, and these are about 3 to 8 inches high.

Other small dolls are used in the Apo ceremonies where the natives dance holding, among various things, two little wooden dolls. The male doll is known as Kwaka and the female as Akua, and they are more in the shape of humans than the flat spade-like dolls of the Ashanti people. Known as the 'speedy messengers of the gods', they can come and go like the wind.

✳   ✳   ✳

Togoland has dolls made from gourds, and also clay dolls with glass eyes. The Bissagoes Islands have large wooden dolls which again are carried on the backs of girls when they are ready for marriage.

Modern dolls in Africa have changed little from the early ones and many of the native dolls decorate the travel shops in the large towns in England.

AFRICA   Key to dolls on page 68

1. Flat wooden doll from Egypt. Grey protruding face, grey bead hair. Body less than $\frac{1}{4}$ in. thick. 2000 B.C. $7\frac{3}{4}$ in. high.　2. Pottery doll found in a grave at Thebes. May be a concubine, as her legs are in one piece to prevent her running away. 1800–1600 B.C.　3. Carved bone doll from Egypt. New Kingdom. 1050 B.C. 4 in. high. British Museum. 4. Blue-glazed doll. Middle Kingdom. 2000 B.C. $3\frac{1}{4}$ in. high. Presented by Lord Carnarvon to the British Museum. 5. Pottery doll, 4 in. high. Pitt Rivers Museum, Dorset.　6. Wooden doll with holes for arms. 1500 B.C. $7\frac{1}{2}$ in. high. Horniman Museum.　7. Carved doll.　8. Coptic doll from Illahun. Wooden, decorated with incised circles. $\frac{1}{4}$ in. thick, $5\frac{1}{8}$ in. high. Pitt Rivers Museum, Oxford.　9. Squeaking doll with bellows-like instrument. 10. Wooden doll with hole possibly to take an offering. Roman period in Thebes. A.D. 100. 6 in. high. British Museum

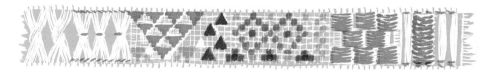

Doll from Las Palmas, Canary Isles
Wool embroidery, muslin blouse, cotton scarf edged with wool, dark brown hair

Boy doll from Casablanca, Morocco

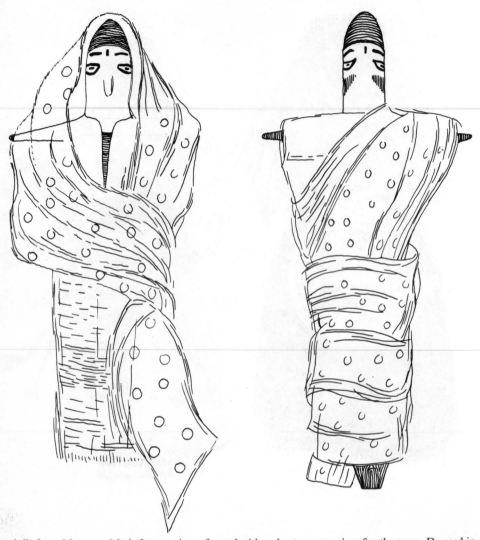

Native dolls from Morocco. Made from a piece of wood with a shorter cross-piece for the arms. Dressed in cream spotted muslin with white dots. Pinkish wool wound around their heads, painted muslin faces, black eyes, fawn cheeks. 7 in. high, 3¾ in. across. Pitt Rivers Museum, Oxford

See opposite page

Doll from Algeria. Dark brown kid, with inset eyes. Navy, red and white woven cloak, raw edge fringe. 15 in. high. Bethnal Green Museum

Modern Egyptian stuffed doll. Plastic head, material body. Brown eyes, pink arms, pale green feet, blue head band with brass ornament, black crêpe dress, stitched to body, black net veil. 9½ in. high. Lent by Miss Juliet Russell

67

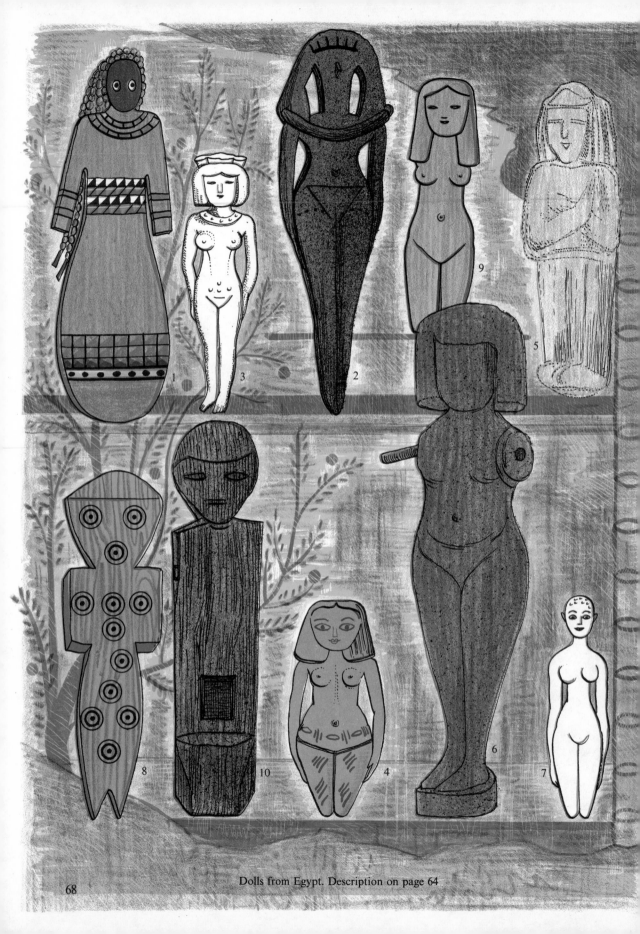

Dolls from Egypt. Description on page 64

Dervish dolls obtained direct from the Omdurman natives
Bodies of stuffed rags. 11 in. high. Pitt Rivers Museum, Oxford

Abyssinian doll with woolly hair and clay beads, showing her construction before dressing

Wooden doll from the Upper Nile. Decorated with hide, cowrie shells, amber beads, dark brown colour, with paler bands. 12 in. high with spear. Horniman Museum

Doll from Wanyika, Uganda. Just a plain wooden doll made from a tree stump, wrapped around with a strip of black cloth edged with beads. 7½ in high. Horniman Museum

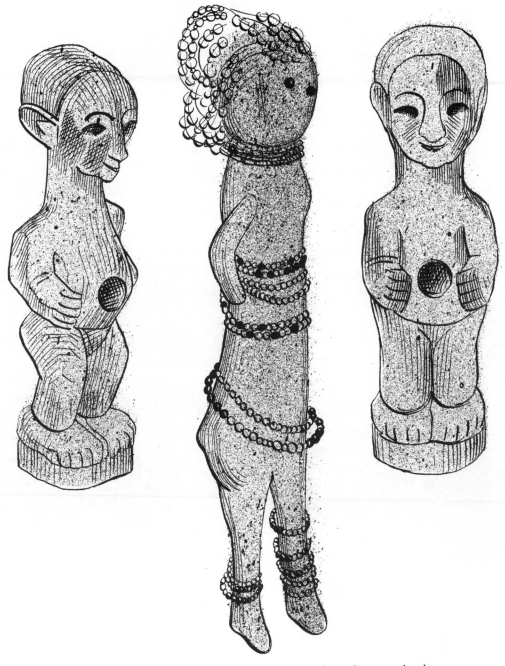

Fetish from the Congo. One of those used by the village doctor for curing stomach-ache

Ba-ila doll from Rhodesia, used in initiation ceremonies. Dark-coloured wood trimmed with beads

Doll from Zanzibar, made of millet stalks and dressed
in a jerkin and beads Nose protrudes ½ in. 8¾ in. high
British Museum

Doll of plaited palm leaves, stuffed with cotton
1914. 10 in. high. Mambrui, Zanzibar. No features indicat
Toy animals are made in the same manner
British Museum

Mohammedan dolls from Mombasa, Kenya.
Bamboo, dressed in beads and printed cotton. 8 in. high
Pitt Rivers Museum, Oxford

73

Doll from Sakalava tribe, Madagascar. Cloth, brown face, black hair, with a similar baby on her back. Yellow cloth, wrapped in white linen. Tucked up inside this doll is a letter with a long list of signatures. 8½ in. high
Pitt Rivers Museum, Oxford

East African doll of fibre and beadwork, gold metal disc for a face without features. Dark brown fibre, pink, blue and white beads, the ends of the fibre forming the hair. 7 in. high. Wellcome Museum, London

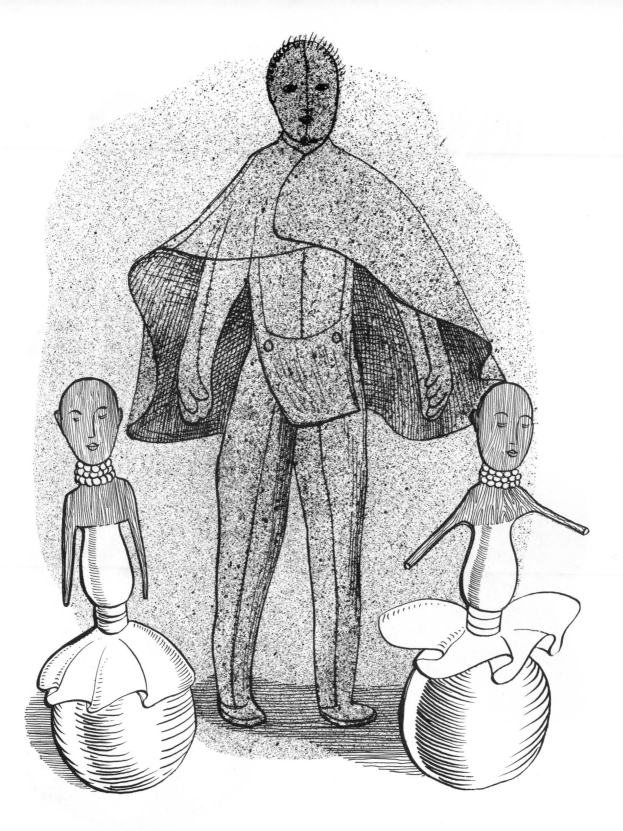

Gourd dolls with dark brown tops and yellow bodies. Decorated with red, white and blue beads

Leather Kaffir doll. Very strong, an Indian red colour all over. Probably represents a Hottentot. 14½ in. high

Pitt Rivers Museum, Oxford

1. Corn-cob doll from the Zulu tribe. 10½ in. high. British Museum
2. Bead doll with clay bead hair
3. Heavy Kaffir doll made of brown wood. 11 in. high. Horniman Museum

See opposite page

1. Doll from Loango, West Africa. Incised markings. When representing a girl a piece of cloth is drawn through the holes at the shoulders, and when a boy the cloth is drawn through the lower holes. 7¾ in. high. Pitt Rivers Museum, Oxford

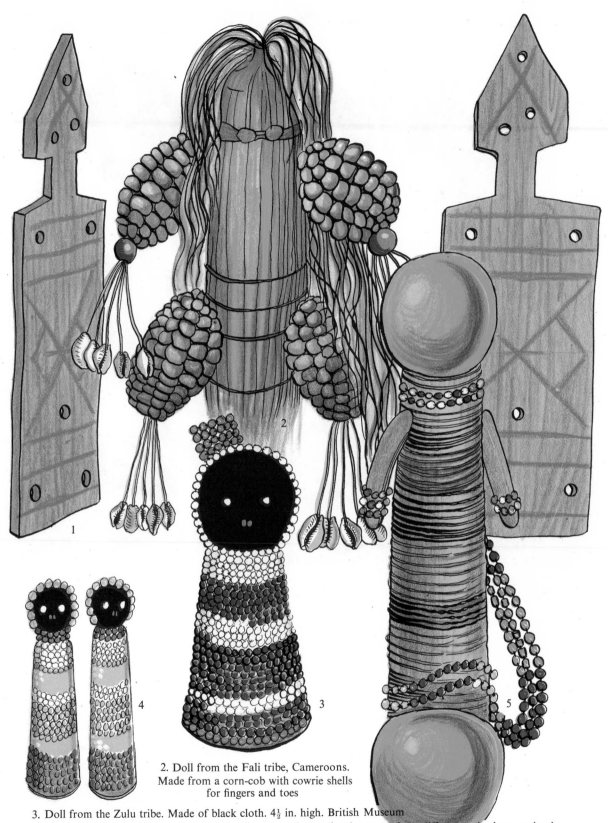

2. Doll from the Fali tribe, Cameroons.
Made from a corn-cob with cowrie shells
for fingers and toes

3. Doll from the Zulu tribe. Made of black cloth. 4½ in. high. British Museum
4. Basuto tribe, twin dolls made from cartridge cases. Interesting because of the different attitudes to twins in
various parts of Africa. 3½ in. high. British Museum
5. Gourd doll bound with string, ornamented with beads. 9 in. high. Bechuanaland. British Museum

Carved wooden doll from Eastern Nigeria. Ibibio tribe, Ikot Ekpene. Pale-coloured wood with black and red markings. A case in the British Museum shows how these dolls are made. 10 in. high

· ♥ · H·R·H · PRINCESS · ANNE · ♥ ·
♥ · FROM · SIR · LADAPO ADEMOLA · K·B·E · C·M·G · THE · ALAKEAB · ♥

Life-size baby doll given to Queen Elizabeth II on the occasion of her visit to Nigeria in 1956. A girl doll for
Princess Anne, a boy doll for her brother. Carved wood with bead cushions. Imperial Institute, London 79

I have never seen a home-made doll, and when I asked our chaps they looked at me blankly. They love European toys if they are ever given them, especially anything mechanical. The girls from five years onwards are responsible for the younger members of the family and carry them around on their backs. When they are about ten years old, they have to help their mothers hoe their plots of land, so I suppose there is no time for dolls and the like (girls are bought at 14 or 15 years as wives).

The boys have a much easier time, they go out to herd the cattle when they are about 8 years, sleeping in the sun, stoning birds from slings, drinking the milk straight from the cows and sheep, etc. When he is 15 years old, he has to start earning his living, generally for a European, until he has enough money to buy himself a wife. Then if he is lazy, he retires to his plot of land and the wife works for him, or if he is ambitious he goes on working until he can afford, first, a bicycle, then a second wife, and then a gramophone, then the third and last wife.
Written to me by Monica Boorer, from Naivasha, Kenya, Africa, 1957

See opposite page
1
Smooth, carved wooden doll with black hair. One of those which are carried on a girl's back to indicate that she is ready for marriage. 18 in. high. Bissagos Island. Wellcome Museum, London
2
Curious stone-coloured figure from West Africa. When a child falls sick, the mother consults the medicine-man, and he tells her where to put this, together with a sacrifice. Wellcome Museum, London
3
Wooden doll covered with a resinous concretion which is often applied to objects used for magical purposes. 13 in. high. Ghana. Wellcome Museum, London
4
Clay doll from Ghana. British Museum

DOLLS OF EUROPE

Most countries have a national or regional dress with a tradition behind it, but dolls throughout the world often have a deeper meaning apart from their clothes.

In the 8th and 9th centuries, rag dolls were mentioned in the *Indiculus Superstitionum*, and dolls were used in connection with black magic, though this is about the only instance where dolls were used for evil purposes.

This sinister custom was prevalent in many places, including parts of England. In Devonshire a doll would be made of wax, quite crude in shape and almost black in colour. Pins and nails were inserted into the vital parts of the doll's body and these were supposed to inflict pains in the corresponding parts of the chosen victim. If death was desired, the doll would be put in the chimney, where the wax melted and the doll wasted away. Evidence of this custom has also been discovered in Belgium and other parts of Europe, indeed, in many parts of the world.

There were other superstitions connected with harvest-time. In England, especially in the West Country, harvest dolls are made, usually from the last gleanings of the field, when the harvest has been gathered in. The last ears of corn are woven together to form a doll, which is then hung up in the homestead in the hope and expectation of a good harvest in the years to come. Last year's doll is taken down and burnt and its spirit is supposed to enter into the new doll. This curious custom also took place in ancient Greece, the doll represented Ceres, the Goddess of Plenty. There are still people who make these dolls, sometimes known as Dollies, in Devon, Cornwall, Somerset and Dorset.

Sometimes a doll would be given to a sick child to serve as a scapegoat, the disease passing from the child into the doll. This same custom prevailed in Celebes, Borneo and other eastern countries.

In England and Germany there were dolls known as 'Changeling Dolls'. These were put in the baby's cradle to deceive fairies and witches, in order that no 'changeling' could be foisted on the parents.

Dolls have also been of use to people who cannot read, or to those speaking a foreign language. They were used as signs outside shops, and hung up to denote the kind of wares one would expect to find inside. An Indian doll denoted the sale of Virginian tobacco, a black doll hung outside a shop denoted produce from West India, including muslin, and marine stores also hung up a doll as a sign. These dolls were often made from curious things, one outside a Portsmouth shop being made from the leg-bone of an ox and draped in old cloth. In Normandy a doll sign indicated a dealer in rags and bones.

'Down Ratcliffe Highway is an old marine store,
And a big black doll hangs out at the door.'
Ingoldsby Legends,
by R. H. Barham, 1788–1845

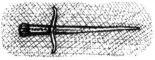

Dagger indicates a wholesale doll manufacturer between 1850–87

In the 1850's, popular gingerbread figures were of the Duke of Wellington. In Yorkshire, dolls are made of bread with currants for eyes and have even been dressed in real clothes. Others are made of bun-dough, have currants for eyes and buttons down their fronts. These can still be bought in many English villages.

At Christmas time, 20th-century children queue up to see dolls arranged in various 'grottos', 'caves', and suchlike, in many of the large London stores. Often these dolls are working models, all of which can be seen after paying a fee, sometimes half-a-crown or more, which is quite a sum if there are many children in one family. The whole set-up is really an inducement to persuade the parent or fond aunt to make purchases for the children, but the scenes are beautifully executed and it is most interesting to watch the different effects which they produce on the young onlookers.

Kate Greenaway dresses 1885

Beginning in the west of Europe, we find that the dolls from Ireland are often dressed as fisher-girls and may carry a basket on their backs; others may have been imported from England, and then clothed in traditional fashion. The modern plastic ones have nylon hair and eyelashes of transparent plastic, and many of these dolls dressed in national costumes have never seen the country they are supposed to have come from. They can be purchased in toyshops, tobacconists' and from street traders, especially near the large railway stations of London and other cities.

In Wales are the same modern dolls, but the larger ones are better made. The small varieties, from 4 to 7 inches high, have plastic faces and rather thick clothes. The larger dolls, about 12 inches high, look much nicer with their blouses, skirts, shawls round their shoulders and tall black hats on their heads. These chimney-pot hats are the most usual, but there are parts of Wales where a flatter, broader hat is also traditional.

It is a curious thing that there is no real national costume of England, but the dresses on the children depicted by Kate Greenaway in the 19th century could be taken as being typical. The girls wear long white dresses with pink or blue sashes, and the boys have short buttoned jackets and long trousers which are buttoned to a silk shirt. These styles are often copied for little bridesmaids and pages at fashionable weddings, but although dolls dressed in these costumes can be seen in museums, they are never seen in the shops. The English dolls in the shops will be representations of John Bull, Guardsmen, Policemen, or Sir Winston Churchill, but these are really mascots and do not rank as dolls in their true sense.

In Scotland there are many dolls dressed in the various tartans; but the origin of the Highland dress is lost in obscurity, the earliest known dating from the end of the 15th century, the kilt arriving at the end of the 16th, and the 'Trews' being for winter use. Highland dress was forbidden except for His Majesty's Forces (George III), between the years 1746 and 1782. Women do not traditionally wear kilts, but nowadays, outside Scotland, they seem to wear them as a kind of fancy dress.

Amongst seafaring folk, if the body of a sailor had been lost at sea, a miniature coffin containing a doll would be used at the funeral ceremony. Small long-shaped boxes with dolls inside have been found near coast towns in France and in 1836 some were found by boys who were playing near King Arthur's Seat in Edinburgh.

✳   ✳   ✳

LAPLAND, NORWAY, SWEDEN AND DENMARK

One of the most well-known persons from this part of Europe played with dolls when he was a boy, his name being Hans Andersen. He used dolls as small actors in his home-made theatres.

'Yes, at that time, though sixteen, I was so childish that I still played with dolls and a dolls' theatre which I made myself. Every day I sat and made dolls' clothes. To get coloured scraps for them, I used to go into shops in Østergade and Kjbømagergade and ask for samples of materials and ribbons. I was so preoccupied with my dolls' dresses that I often stood in the streets watching the rich ladies in their silks and velvets and imagining all the kings' cloaks, trains and knightly costumes my scissors could snip out of their finery.'

The Swedish film-star, Greta Garbo, had few dolls or toys when she was a small girl, but as soon as she could afford it, some of the first things she purchased were dolls. This collection of dolls she kept for a number of years, but eventually the whole crate-full was sold in an auction sale for thirty kroner, less than two pounds, because she asked that the identity of the owner be kept a secret. Had anyone known whose dolls they were, they would have fetched much more money.

The dolls from Lapland have jet-black hair with thick fringes and perhaps two long tails at the back, and they are dressed in furs and pieces of reindeer skin. The dolls dressed in the traditional costumes of Sweden, Norway and Denmark mostly have fair hair and blue eyes, and in Finland there are still carved wooden dolls to be found. There is a shop in Helsinki which has dolls in national costume.

Dolls made from birch-bark are a novelty from Sweden, but in the museums many of the dolls are much the same as we have in England. The wooden stump dolls were made in Denmark from about A.D. 1610, and china dolls representing Jenny Lind, the Swedish singer, were popular about 1852.

Miniature dolls depicting the bride and groom were used as decorations on wedding confections, just as in England during the reign of Queen Victoria, and also in the U.S.A. In Denmark this custom still prevails and many of the modern dolls are made from wire and bound around entirely with wool. Beautifully made, they are from 4 to 6 inches high.

Small dolls, well dressed in traditional costumes, are made by Lisbeth Lind and are for sale in Copenhagen.

✳   ✳   ✳

THE NETHERLANDS

A kind of white magic persisted in Belgium in order to help an infant cut its teeth without pain or danger of fits. A doll, dressed in swathing bands, would have a human molar tooth attached to it with a safety-pin. This doll was given to the baby about the time when it was due to cut its teeth. The dead tooth was supposed to act as a charm.

Black magic also was practised with the aid of dolls, in the manner described in England.

The most well-known dolls from these parts are those known as Flanders babies. These 'Dutch' dolls, made entirely of wood, were popular in England, in fact all over the civilized world during the 18th, 19th and early part of the 20th centuries. There are just a few in some of the English shops today.

They are jointed dolls, the number of joints depending on the price and size. On the cheaper dolls these joints would be at the shoulders and thighs only, but on the better kind also at the elbows and the knees. Even the very tiny ones were jointed, measuring half an inch, or three-quarters of an inch, or an inch high; sometimes three of them would be contained in a small wooden egg. These little eggs could be purchased for sixpence just before the 1939 war.

The dolls' arms perform a forward movement at the shoulders, and the heads rarely turn, being in one with the neck and shoulders. The features are painted; sometimes the eyes are rather close together, giving a grumpy expression, but the wider apart eyes give the dolls a cheerful look, with their nice pink cheeks, small mouths and black shiny hair. Always black; I have never seen a fair-haired 'Dutch' doll, and yet the eyes can be black, brown or forget-me-not blue, and always with eyebrows made with sweeping strokes of black paint. The nose is indicated by paint on the smaller dolls, but on the larger variety a little wedge of wood is inserted in order to give a perky prominent feature. The upper parts of these dolls are turned on a lathe.

Small dolls make suitable occupants of dolls' houses, and they are often dressed as maids wearing caps and aprons, or as nurses in the nursery at the top of the house. Sometimes a little hair would be gummed to the wooden heads under the caps. Such a maid lives in the doll's house burgled by the two bad mice in the story by Beatrix Potter.

Dolls like these Flanders babies are made today in Germany and northern Italy. The arms are inset rather low, giving a broad-shoulder effect, very different from the beautiful little ones made during the reign of Queen Victoria and at the beginning of the 19th century. The carving is usually done by the men and boys and the colouring left to the womenfolk. Today a 6-inch high doll sells for one and sixpence and those of about 10 inches tall, for about three shillings and sixpence.

I quote here a letter from the Openair Folk Museum at Arnhem:

'The "Dutch" dolls were not made in Holland. They were only used in our country. We imported these dolls from the woody borderland of Germany and Czechoslovakia, especially from Bohemia.

Leather or textile was used for the joints of arms and legs of the oldest dolls. Perhaps the name "Dutch dolls" is caused by the Dutch name for Germany. We do not speak of German but of "Duits". In Holland the dolls mentioned above are called "Duitse poppen". You will see the resemblance of the English Dutch and our Duits.'

J. De Kleyn. Ethnol. Drs. Rijksmuseum voor Volkskunde

In Flanders, Father Christmas rides on a horse, but in Holland he comes in a boat with his bag of toys. In Germany he often carries a birch for the naughty children, as a warning that they may not get any presents, and the same custom happens in the Netherlands.

Rotterdam is a good shopping centre for playthings, and dolls dressed in traditional costumes can cost seventy shillings or more, but there are many well-dressed small dolls in regional clothes.

*　　　　*　　　　*

FRANCE

Here, in some of the coast towns, small dolls in coffins have also been discovered. At the island of Ushant these were used at the church service and afterwards placed in a vault near the patron saint of seamen, in place of the sailor's body if it had been lost at sea. By 1912, a small cross was used instead of the figure of a doll. Also, in France, a small 'spirit' doll has been found similar to those used in the Congo.

The earliest mention of an ivory doll in France was in the 14th century, when a doll was unearthed at a depth of 40 feet, from the banks of the River Vezère.

In 1391, dolls were sent from here to the young queen of England, primarily to display the fashions, and were full-size models. On her marriage to Charles VI, Queen Isabelle of Bavaria introduced dolls to the French court. These were expensive dolls, those for the Queen of England costing over 459 livres, according to Robert de Varennes, embroiderer and valet to the French King.

By the middle of the 15th century, dolls were noted for being 'charming and beautifully dressed' and it is for their clothes that the dolls from France have become famous.

Amongst the royal family even the grown-ups had dolls, and in the time of the Valois a doll would wear a beautiful dress of flowered white silk, trimmed with orange embroidery. Henri II of France bought six dolls in Paris for his wife, the grand dolls being individually carved in wood. There were cheaper dolls made from pasteboard and pressed in moulds, and the expensive kind were also equipped with toilet articles, wardrobes and beds.

We are told by Fournier in 1889 that in France from the 14th to the 18th centuries a doll, no longer a little girl's doll, but a doll of a fine size, a well brought-up doll, grown up, a woman of the world – was sent in her best clothes from the town where the fashions made the laws – in fact this package was always sent from Paris to cities less privileged (but no less populated with pretty vain women) where one wished to be quickly initiated into the novelties of dress and to know the very latest word of the present fashion.

Franisque Michel says:
We can compare with these little masterpieces the exquisite thing which Tallemant des Reaux mentions in his anecdote about the famous minister of Louis XIII. 'The Cardinal', he says, 'gave Mme d'Enghien a little room in which there were six dolls – . . . and the grandmother Mlle de Rambouillet, Mademoiselle de Bouteville and others played with her (Mme d'Enghien). Every evening they undressed and put to bed the dolls. The next day they dressed them again – gave them meals and made them take medicine. One day she wanted to bath them, and they had great difficulty in preventing her doing so.'

Fashion dolls were the general practice in France before the coming of mannequins, and the dolls made as playthings were of various materials. Wooden, rag and stuffed dolls were all for sale and there were shops in the rue St Denis where dolls could be purchased. Dolls had carved wooden hands stuffed up the sleeves of their gowns as in England.

While imprisoned in the Temple, Marie Antoinette dressed a doll for her daughter, and this doll, together with sets of clothes, can be seen in the museum at Salisbury, in Wiltshire, England. Many years later 'Odette' made dolls when imprisoned by the Nazis and from time to time these are shown at exhibitions.

The dolls dressed as aristocrats disappeared during the time of the French Revolution, some even having their heads chopped off by toy guillotines, but when all this was over, dolls appeared expensively dressed in the fashions of the Empire. Some were attended by running footmen, others were made to ride horseback, many of them being imported from Germany but dressed in France.

Doll with clothes made by Marie Antoinette for her daughter, while in prison. Salisbury Museum

During the reign of Louis XVIII, there was a rhyme concerning the making of a trousseau for a well-dressed doll.

France had to pay heavy duty on the dolls imported from England and Germany, but in the 19th century, Monsieur Jumeau made beautiful dolls' heads of wax and of bisque. Usually heads were hollow so that they weighed less, and were sometimes filled with cork, though some were found stuffed with contraband goods in order to evade customs duty between various countries.

Dolls were made of ten pieces. Paste or wax head and shoulders, lambskin bodies stuffed with sawdust, enamel or straw teeth, glass or enamel eyes, wooden or skin or paste hands, a wig, stockings, complete wardrobe, hat or shoes. This was in 1849.

Many of the dolls were dressed at home, but shops sold clothes separately from the dolls. In 1909, dolls' gloves and shoes of various sizes could be purchased in the rue St Honoré, Paris, at the 'Nain Bleu'.

In 1923, fashionable Parisian women took dolls with them on their strolls, and many grotesque dolls belong to this period. They were more decorations than playthings, and were often made by French ladies for pin-money, especially by those who had been wealthy before the 1914–18 War.

In the Musée des Arts Décoratifs are modern dolls dressed in historical costume, depicting ladies of the French courts.

Today in England French dolls are popular, the latest kind having wonderful hair which can be washed, complete with their own shampoos, eyes to open and shut and, of course, long eyelashes. These can be bought for about forty-five shillings in London, and in the 'boutiques' of France, dolls are sold dressed in the various costumes which are peculiar to the different provinces. Present-day manufacturers are the Poupées Bella, 193 Avenue de Rivesaltes, Perpignan (Pyr-Or), France.

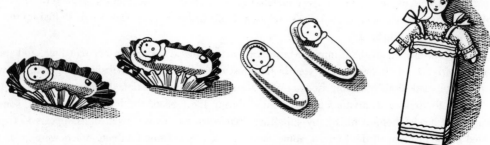

A box of sugared almonds for a present at christening ceremonies. Designed by Egrefeuil in 1865

SPAIN AND PORTUGAL

If a baby should die, the custom of having a wax effigy made in the likeness of the child was sometimes followed in these countries, as in other parts of Europe and in South America. The noble lady, living in a grand house, would commission the wax doll to be made full size, and she would dress it in the baby's own clothes and also lay it in the cradle. Such a doll as this is in the Victoria and Albert Museum, and if it is not on show, it is wise to ask for a peep at it, because the white robes are beautifully embroidered in white threads in typical Portuguese designs, and the wax baby itself is well worth studying.

The dressed Spanish dolls have lace mantillas and miniature combs, and the men dolls are often dressed in the traditional clothes seen in the bull-rings. Dolls dressed as aristocrats or as peasants can be bought in the shops, the most well-known modern ones being those made by Mariquita Pérez in Madrid. Some modern dolls here are made much like the ones found in South America, that is on a wire foundation and with swirling skirts often covered with embroidery. Dolls can also be purchased unclothed and the various items of their wardrobes chosen separately.

Tumbler dolls, or tilting toys, very often resemble monks or nuns.

Details from the robe of a wax doll, a life-size wax effigy from Portugal. Victoria and Albert Museum, London

ITALY

Many of the early Roman dolls which were made of wood have, of course, perished, but a jointed wooden doll nearly a foot high was found in a Roman tomb and on the doll were traces of gilding. A wooden comb, silver mirror and other toilet articles were also in good preservation, and this custom of burying playthings with their little owners has given people a good idea of the dolls of the past. The same thing was done in England during the Roman occupation and a small doll found at Sandy, in Bedfordshire, England, has neither arms nor legs, and is obviously a plaything.

Dolls made of bone and of ivory have been found in the catacombs, and carving dolls for the children must have been one way of amusing them when the early Christians were in hiding during their persecutions. Some of these dolls were jointed at the thighs, the upper legs being fixed to the rather square bodies with wire or string.

Quite elaborate head-dresses were carved on some of the early Roman dolls, especially those of bone or ivory, and by the end of the 4th century A.D. there was much trade in these playthings. Some were carved by hand, others were made in moulds and some stood on small wooden bases.

After her first child was born, it was the custom for a mother to hang up a doll in the temple, together with other offerings, these dolls being quite small and sometimes bearing a likeness to the new baby. A Roman child would play with her dolls until her marriage; then she would dedicate them solemnly to Venus or to Artemis, together with her other playthings. This must have been very hard on the children, especially as they were married at an early age.

The custom of throwing a child in the River Tiber, at certain times of the year, was ended by the substitution of a doll. This doll was made of plaited rushes. Another survival of pagan times was the placing of a coin in the foundation stone of buildings, where, in other parts, a doll had been substituted. We English children, knowing nothing whatever of ancient burial customs, buried balls and bones in the grave of our dead dog, just as the Romans did in the graves of the children.

In Sorrento there is a wooden doll known as a Lent doll. Rather similar to a 'Dutch' doll, but with carved hair, she has her legs fixed into a wooden ball, or an apple or an orange. In this ball are placed six black feathers and one white one pointing downwards. The six black feathers represent the six weeks of Lent, one being pulled out every week, until finally, on Easter Day, the white one is taken out. Italian hotels hang these dolls up at this time of the year, and as the feathers are pulled out, week by week, they are often burnt for luck.

Present-day dolls, dressed in the traditional costumes of the various regions, can be purchased in the towns, or even in London, but they are rather expensive as toys.

It is interesting that in Malta the dolls all bear the names of saints.

Regional doll, 8" high.

Wooden dolls from Lake Como, Italy. Jointed, painted and varnished. 1¾ in. high. Lent by Mrs Harrison

✳   ✳   ✳

GERMANY

Many of the playthings of Germany have been mentioned in early writings and illustrated by woodcuts. These show wooden dolls being carved, and clay dolls in the process of moulding and being fired in kilns, apart from portraits of children playing with dolls or holding them in their hands.

The carved wooden dolls, known as Tocken or Docken, were made by peasants during the winter months, and brought into the markets for sale. The districts around Nuremberg and Sonneberg were well known for these carved toys.

A German writer mentioned dolls in the 12th century A.D. and a preacher in the town of Strasbourg commented on parents who taught children to be proud of their dolls. In the 15th century, Martin Luther rebuked women for dressing themselves up to look like 'pretty Tocken', and much the same kind of thing happened in England at this time, the expression of being 'dolled up' having something to do with the many ribbons and laces the women wore.

The white clay dolls, with a flat hollowed circle in the front, show where christening money was put when these dolls were given as presents. Wooden dolls, carved by the peasants, at first were shaped like ninepins, having neither arms nor legs and their features indicated by paint.

From Brunswick come flax dolls, sometimes made in pairs, a boy and a girl, these being for the purpose of bringing luck to the house. They were hung on spinning wheels. Newly married couples living in the Austrian forests were presented with small dolls lying in cots, and figures of Saint Nicholas made in gingerbread were presented to children on his feast day. In Germany, Father Christmas rides in a sleigh, accompanied by his servant, Rupprecht. Rupprecht does the dirty work, he climbs down the chimneys and carries a birch for the naughty children, and some children may be terrified by his nasty face as he and Father Christmas tour the villages at Christmas time. When the children have promised to be good, Father Christmas comforts them and gives them presents. These two figures are often made as dolls or as smaller figures for confectionery.

A doll wearing a rich costume and a bride's crown is known as a 'Nürnberger Kronbraut'. The Dauphin, in France, had dolls sent to him from Germany for three years running; in 1604 he was given a pasteboard man, in 1605 a clay one and the next year a little man who was 'well-dressed'.

In 1750, some of the eyes for dolls were made from Steigel glass, and early in the 19th century, papier-mâché dolls were made in sulphur moulds and were exported from Sonneberg in great quantities. After the

Two flax dolls from Brunswick, a girl and a boy
It was the custom to hang these on a spinning-wheel for luck

year 1891, all dolls imported into England had to be marked with the country of their origin. This stamped or engraved mark is usually found on the back of the doll's neck or just under the hair.

Dolls like the 'Flanders Babies' have been made in Germany during the 18th century, especially in the Black Forest areas and in the northern part of Italy, and these are exported even today, but not in such large quantities as in former years.

The tilting toy in Germany is known as a 'Pulzelmann'. In December the famous Kris Kringle Fair is held at Nuremberg, and visitors come from all over the world. There are wonderful hand-carved wooden dolls and toys, in true folk tradition, and also mechanical ones, at the Toy Trade Fair in March.

There is an attractive story about the first Christmas angel of Nuremberg, which goes as follows:

Mr Hauser, the dollmaker, had a beautiful little daughter, but one year, just before Christmas, she died. He and his wife were heavy with sorrow and Mr Hauser was so heartbroken that he could not work. He walked the long narrow streets of Nuremberg late into the night, wondering how he could comfort his wife, who was ill with grief. One night as he lay awake he suddenly had an idea and he got up and crept silently down to his workshop, and began to chip and carve, and carve and smooth, until he had made a figure like an angel, with a golden robe and a crown upon her head. He carried the precious thing to his sleeping wife and laid it in her arms. She stirred and opened her eyes; 'Why, it looks just like our little girl,' she said, and smiled.

When their neighbours saw the angel they asked Mr Hauser to carve them one as well, and he began to work happily again and made many little golden angels to sell at the Christmas Fair. Now over three hundred years have passed, and from all over the world people come to buy the 'Rauchsgoldengel' at the 'Christkindlersmarktes'.

✳ SWITZERLAND ✳

On Shrove Tuesday, a masked fool carries a doll to the newly married couples, in some of the mountain districts.

Mechanical dolls are made here, which are sometimes real dolls, but often they are made to stand on the top of a musical box. These figures dance to a national tune, to the latest 'hit' from a play or to a waltz from Germany. There are some very large dolls standing on top of musical boxes in a shop south of the British Museum, known as Cameo Corner. These were given to the owners of the shop by Queen Mary, and anyone may inspect them but they are not for sale.

Other dolls are made from material and stuffed, and these can be purchased in Switzerland dressed in traditional costumes, like other dolls from European countries.

To the east of Switzerland, in the Tyrol, dolls are made representing Saint Nicholas and a figure known as Krampus. Krampus is black, with two long horns, and looks rather like a devil. In his hand he carries a two-pronged fork.

Krampus, like Rupprecht, birches naughty children, but Saint Nicholas comforts them, after they have begged forgiveness, by giving them presents of iced cakes and sweets. Boys dress up representing these two characters, and on the eve of St Nicholas, December 5th, they call at the houses where children live.

✳ AUSTRIA ✳

In the forest districts of Austria, the peasants sometimes present a newly married couple with a doll lying in a cot. This doll is crudely made and quite small, but the gift is intended to bring good luck and a plenteous family.

Modern dolls of a Viennese character can be purchased in Vienna, and one of the shops is known as the 'Puppenparadies', that is, the Dolls' Heaven.

✳ YUGOSLAVIA ✳

In Belgrade there is a custom of putting a doll in the window of a house in which lives a marriageable girl and this doll is dressed as a bride. Sometimes a doll might be put in a window of a house where there are no children.

Dolls play quite an important part in the regions of Upper Moravia, Czechoslovakia, each doll having a particular function. One may be the mother, or the mother-in-law. Another the second daughter, or third daughter-in-law and so on, each doll being named after a certain member of the family.

GREECE

In the centuries before the birth of Christ, Greece was the centre of the doll trade, just as in later years the home of dolls was in Germany. Even during the 5th and 4th centuries B.C., there were dolls with movable arms and legs. They were beautifully modelled, mostly in terra-cotta, but there were ivory dolls also, and dolls of wood which have perished with time.

Some dolls of even earlier date show a distinct Egyptian influence, and during the 6th and 5th centuries the bodies show traces of paint. These early Greek dolls have been found in graves, buried with their small owners, and this accounts for their good preservation. Hippodamia, the daughter of Œnomaus, had a doll's bed, which she offered up to Jupiter Olympus at Elis. In a tomb at Athens many miniature objects were found, such as a marriage bowl, shoes and an object used for spinning. The Greek girls of all ages played with dolls, and their dolls' rooms were complete with clay furniture. The British Museum, London, possessed some of these 'doll's houses', but unfortunately they have been destroyed.

As long ago as the time of Plato, 427–347 B.C., men were compared with the movable strings of a doll. Aristotle says, 'See those who represent, by means of wooden figures, men and their gestures. They pull a thread, corresponding to the limb they wish to move, the head makes a sign, the eyes turn, the hands perform the desired act, and the whole represents well enough a human being.' This mention of the turning of the eyes is very interesting and also the turning of the head, because most of the small dolls which have been found have the head, neck and body carved in one piece.

The movable dolls were usually jointed at the shoulders and at the thighs, but some have been found with a knee joint. The base of the body was carved out to take the thigh joint, which was attached with cords, similar to the manner in which the shoulders were also jointed. Sometimes the thread came out through the top of the head, thus enabling the figures to jump about.

Sardis, the capital of Lydia, was a centre for playthings, and from here came many terra-cotta dolls and toy animals, which were sold in the market places, laid out on stalls in the streets.

Plutarch had a small daughter, who died when she was two years old. This little girl asked her nurse to feed her doll as well as her playmates. When Sappho dedicated her doll to Venus, she said 'Do not disdain the purple draperies of my doll', so these Greek children clothed their dolls also, but these robes have perished.

None of the wax dolls of ancient Greece have survived, but Callimachus compared Erisichthon to a doll which melted in the sun, during the 2nd century B.C. Daedalus, the father of Icarus, is said to have made a wooden statue of Venus, and made it move by pouring liquid silver into it. This invention could almost be the forerunner of the modern tilting toy, or tumbler doll.

A kind of clown doll was made, in the form of a hunchback, black in colour and this sometimes had a protruding tummy instead of a humped back.

✳   ✳   ✳

Modern dolls, man 9" high woman 8". lent by Mrs Bishop.

RUSSIA

This country is another home for hand-made dolls, mostly carved of wood and often with ingenious wooden joints. Made by peasants during the hard winter months, the dolls would sometimes be carved for their own children, but more often taken to the markets for sale when the spring came.

Other early dolls are the Woodmen Dolls, made from blocks of wood and with painted faces, and the Moss Men and Women. These are made from moss, wood, and string which is bound round the moss and the dolls are fitted into wooden stands. Two of these dolls are in the Pitt Rivers Museum at Oxford, with a letter attached to them:

I am sending the dear Uncle for New Year, a little Russian Moss Man, made in the far 'districts' where the forest-god rules in the natives' hearts till now. He used to be worshipped under this prin, so I have got one sent, on the chance Uncle has not seen one. The arm being of pine-cone is a particular point, the Russians say. I thought New Year would be the right time as he isn't a bit of a Christian, he guarded the forests from time immemorial. I thought the poor man looked so forlorn without his wife that I have sent her too.

Juliet Morse, 14 Airlie Gardens, London. Dec. 27th, 1909

(I do not know what a 'prin' could be, but it may be principality.)

Straw dolls of Slav origin symbolize Winter's death, made of plaited straw and empty ears of wheat. Tiny figures of mint-bread are made for hanging on Christmas trees, and Nest Dolls are made in Russia and surrounding countries. In all Slav countries, red is the favourite colour and black comes second. The chicken and the grape emblems represent fertility, and these motifs are traditional.

In the old days, many of the large houses had nurseries as in England, and dolls richly clad have found their way into the museums as in other parts of the world. The dolls were contemporary with ours, having wooden, wax or china heads.

A mint-bread doll, for decorating a Christmas-tree
Figure of plaited straw, and with empty ears of wheat.
Known as 'Winter's Death'. It is of Slav origin

Two Russian dolls from Moscow. Painted wood. Early 19th century. 6½ in. high

Queer tree roots, resembling human shapes, were used as witches' dolls in Poland. Quite grotesque-looking, these were far removed from dolls as playthings, and were known as the 'Familiar Spirits of Witches'.

Russia is famous for the Nest dolls. The large doll opened in half, around the waist, revealing a slightly smaller doll, which in turn opened to show yet another doll, and this would continue until the smallest doll, scarcely half an inch high, would appear. The number of dolls in a Nest Doll depended on the size of the first one. If this was about 9 inches high, there might be as many as fifteen dolls fitted snugly inside, each one being slightly smaller than the previous one, and coloured in a different way.

Some Nest dolls, when opened, might contain six small tumbler dolls of the same size, three with red scarves, three with yellow, painted round their necks. A man doll, when opened, might contain a set of ninepins with two wooden balls, and all of these would be turned from wood, painted and highly varnished.

As the U.S.S.R. is so large, the dolls from Siberia will be found in the section on Asia.

In her book *Mirror to Russia*, Marie Noelle Kelly has an interesting paragraph on dolls.

There are other things to buy in the Kolkhoz, . . . here, too, are those traditional wooden dolls some of us remember from childhood, painted with gay brilliant colours and solemn flat faces, which unscrew in the middle to reveal yet another and another doll-within-doll. . . . Zagorsk Museum, modern Russian toys, all very pleasing and original, even if a little childish. . . . The toys which come from the local handicraft centre and which are the town's principal industry, though produced in quantity, are hand-made in the old tradition, and are sold all over Russia. The soft unpainted white wooden ones, mostly farm animals, are charming. In this museum the dolls, the duga, and the bats for beating linen are the most typical and ornamental examples of peasant art.   1952

✳   ✳   ✳

In Finland and all around here, indeed almost everywhere, plastic dolls are gradually taking the place of these beautiful hand-made toys, but beautiful dolls, well dressed in traditional clothes, are still to be found by hunting for them. Dolls dressed in national costume can be bought in Helsinki

"Polly Jones
Licensed Hawker 109"
54 articles in basket

Pedlar doll
about 1800
Exeter Museum, Devonshire

96

Doll dressed in Irish costume. Black-and-white check blouse, red flannel skirt with black braid, fawn neckerchief and blue apron. Modern doll, flesh-coloured composition, jointed. Strip of blue perspex on top lid which is in one with the eyeball, enabling the eyes to open and shut. Glistening eyes of paperweight variety. Stands erect on her own with head large in proportion to the body. Many modern dolls conform to this type. Across the waist at the back are the words 'Made in England'. Head $2\frac{1}{4}$ in. high, total height $7\frac{1}{4}$ in. Lent by Miss Sheila Ashe

Welsh doll, 1889. Wax face, wearing a tweed dress and woven apron, black shoes with brown heels. Her name is Jenny Morgan. In the same museum is Betty Jones who wears a wider hat with a lower crown. Both hats are typical in Wales, though the taller one is well known. 16 in. high. Tenby Museum, South Wales

Modern English doll, 1959, again showing large heads on modern dolls. 16 in. high, face 3 in. to the hair. A Pedigree doll called 'Julia', she is lent by Miss Cherry Graham Scott

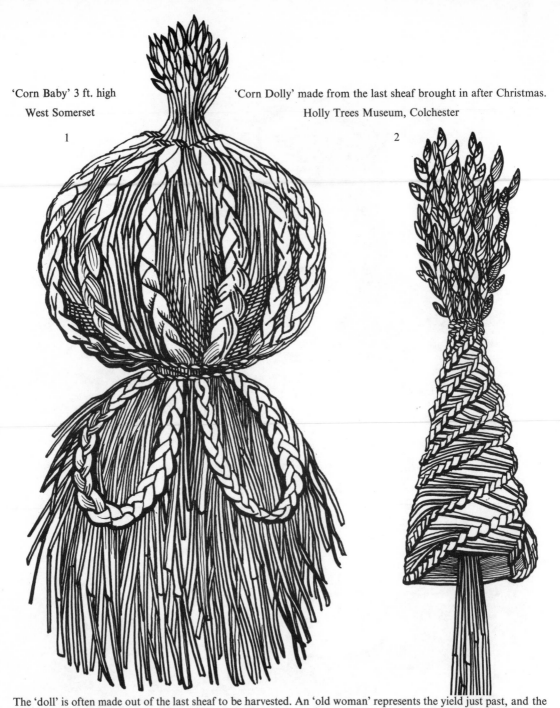

'Corn Baby' 3 ft. high
West Somerset

1

'Corn Dolly' made from the last sheaf brought in after Christmas.
Holly Trees Museum, Colchester

2

The 'doll' is often made out of the last sheaf to be harvested. An 'old woman' represents the yield just past, and the 'maiden' the hoped-for harvest. In Scotland, the old woman is called the 'Carline'. Often the doll is taken to the farmhouse and fastened to the wall. In the Hebrides, it is sometimes taken at night and put in the field of a lazy farmer. In Belfast the last sheaf is called the 'Granny', while in Germany it is known as the 'Oats Bride' or 'Wheat Bride', and in Bulgaria the corn dolly may be known as the Corn Queen or Corn Mother

100

1. Early 19th-century wooden doll, red painted shoes. Dressed in white with black sash. 6 in. high
Aylesbury Museum, Buckinghamshire

2.
Wax penny doll, 1840, wearing coarse yellow muslin dress, pale green sash, trimmed with blue bands, cream lace.
Straw hat bound with primrose coloured material. 6 in. high
Given by Mrs Burgess to Gunnersbury Museum, Middlesex

3. Two drawings of 'Julia'

Wooden doll dressed in cotton, wearing a lace cap. 6½ in. high. Lent by Mrs Nerea de Clifford

English wax doll, 1844, with wax head and arms, wearing a dress and cape of 'Broderie Anglaise'
Given by Queen Mary to the Bethnal Green Museum

white→

white   red red red   white   red red red

navy   red   green

Doll in Highland dress. China head and hair (bisque), pink kid body wearing the tartan of the Frazer clan, green bows, brown velvet jacket, navy velvet cap. About 1870. 11 in. high with rather a small head. London Museum, Kensington Palace

Three dolls from Lapland, with fringes of jet-black hair and pigtails. Dressed in reindeer skins, one in winter garb, two in summer clothes

Doll with drawn-thread apron, from Norway

Modern doll from Denmark dressed in regional costume

Doll from Denmark. 1930. Composition head, stuffed body, flesh-coloured arms and red stockings. Skirt material folded double at the hem and gathered at the waist. Cross-over bodice and sash, two fair-haired plaits. 7 in. high
Brought from Denmark for me by my brother

Dutch dolls from the province of Zeeland
Victoria and Albert Museum

Birch-bark doll from Sweden

NI435E
Handmalad
Väund
Smål.

Wooden doll from Sweden, woolly hair, movable arms. 4½ in. high. Lent by Miss Julia Harrison

French doll, composition face, painted features, kid body and hands. A very stiff, starched petticoat under her dark blue silk dress. Hat of wire and net trimmed with cream ribbon. 13 in. high. Bethnal Green Museum

Woven
socks

Brown leather
shoes with buckles

Pale mauve flowers
with purple stem

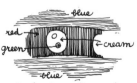

blue
red
green
cream
blue

Underdress trimmed
with braid

French doll from Paris. 1869. Wax with inset hair. Dressed in a sprigged frock over a bright blue underdress. Cotton socks, brown leather shoes with buckles. Gunnersbury Museum, Middlesex

Doll from Cannes. A typical celluloid doll of the present day, hair fixed with gum. FRANCE 130 marked on back of neck. Dressed in printed cotton skirt, net sleeves, painted apron, straw hat. 6½ in. high. These little dolls are often used as window displays. Lent by Miss Julia Harrison

110

cardboard
sole
scale one inch

Typical modern doll from Genoa, Italy, dressed in regional costume. Composition head, stuffed muslin arms, large black shoes with cardboard soles, long white knickers edged with lace, plain white petticoat. 8 in. high.
Lent by Miss Julia Harrison

Modern doll from Catalonia, Spain, made of cloth over a wire foundation stuffed with seeds. 10 in. high.
Lent by Miss Rosemary Harrison

Early jointed doll from Spain

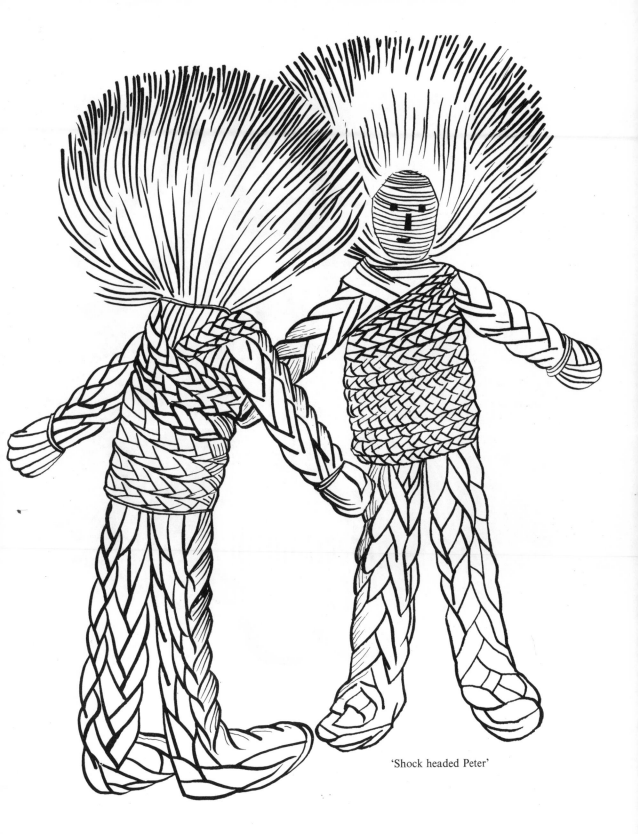

'Shock headed Peter'

Doll from Austria, made of straw, plaited, straw hair, black eyes, nose, red mouth, cheeks, blue raffia jersey, arms bound in red at the wrists. 15 in. high. Bethnal Green Museum

Sole of shoe

Modern doll from Liguria, Italy. Composition head, nylon hair, soft plastic hands, red plastic shoes, with the name ROSY stamped on the heels. Dressed in felt and cotton. $8\frac{1}{2}$ in. high. Lent by Miss Rosemary Harrison

Modern Swiss doll, celluloid, jointed, imitation hair with parting continuing to back of head. Tortoise in diamond shape on back of neck. 7¾ in. high. Lent by Miss Julia Harrison

Roman rag doll. 6½ in. high. British Museum
(I have drawn him many times, but
he seems to be 'the one and only')

Doll from Sorrento, Italy, 1904. This is a Lent doll, showing black feathers with a white one for Easter. 8 in. high
Pitt Rivers Museum, Oxford

Doll from Switzerland. Bisque head, blue eyes, real hair, flat wooden hands made all in one. Dressed in a black gown, black lace mittens, filigree ornaments and chain, pale green hat. 12 in. high. Bethnal Green Museum

German doll dressed as a maidservant. 1880. Wax head and shoulders, real hair wig, wax arms, pale blue glass eyes. White flannel petticoat, long white drawers, woven socks with red pattern at the top. Black shoes with silver buckles, metal heels. Blue glass earrings. 10 in. high. Bethnal Green Museum

Doll with tin head, white calico body, kid arms. Given to St Albans Museum, England, by Mrs Pitt of New York State. Wearing clothes made by Mrs Tonkers, chemise, knickers, salmon-pink dress, flat black shoes, white cotton socks. Doll 21 in. high. On undressing this doll, I found the mark DIANA, 8, dep, DRGM 160633. The letters DRGM mean that she was made in Germany

1. Wooden doll, with tooth attached,
   to assist a baby when teething
   Belgium   2. Bavarian stump dolls

3. Painted doll. Folk Museum, Cambridge

4. Coptic doll of woo
   from France
   600 B.C.

6. An early doll from Greece   8. Polished wooden doll, from Lithuania

7. German stump doll, 14th century   9. Baby-doll, carved in maple-wo

5. Bronze doll from Germany, 700 B.C.   5½ in. high   16 in. high. Czechoslovakia

Small

Woman doll from Bosnia

Man and woman doll from Bosnia, Jugoslavia
Flocked faces over papier mâché masks, stuffed heads with
woolly hair, painted features. Dressed in thick material.
Woman has a woven shopping-bag

Given by Mrs Rudoi to the
Bethnal Green Museum

124

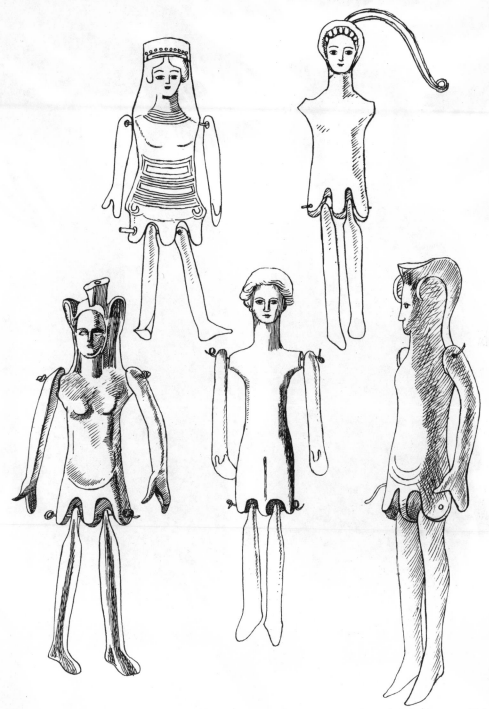

Clay dolls from Greece. They show the manner in which the limbs were jointed, heads being in one with bodies Mostly a pinkish or an ochre colour. 4 to 6 in. high. British Museum

Russian Moss man and Moss woman. Made of moss with plaited shoes and bark hat. Woman has fir-cone arm and a bundle of sticks. 10 in. high. Pitt Rivers Museum, Oxford

Russian Nest dolls. The men sometimes have ninepins and wooden balls inside

127

Ushabti figure found in Cyprus. Used about 2466 B.C. until Roman times, 30 B.C. Found in 1890 by Colonel Nash, and on loan to the Chelmsford and Essex Museum

Afghan doll from Kabul. Stuffed body, features worked in silk. Black sleeves sewn to yoke, skirt lightly pleated, all sewn by hand and stitched to the body. Machine stitched braid, and metal discs. Brought back by an English author who had difficulty in obtaining it. 18 in. high, head 4 in. high, width across from finger tips 16 in. Lent by Miss Juliet Russell

Doll from Jordan, one of those made by refugees in the camps today. 7 in. high. Lent by Miss Gollmick

AQABATJABER Refugee Camp. The World's Y.W.C.A. School, Jericho.

The Arab refugees make dolls for sale, the money goes towards their upkeep. If anyone wants to buy a doll by post, a cheque can be sent, as it is a sterling country. The address for these dolls is: Miss J. Awad, Y.W.C.A., Herod's Gate, Jerusalem, Jordan. Each one is authentic for the local costumes and every one is different, as is the case with most hand-made articles. They cost about 8s. 6d. to 12s. 6d. and are about 7 in. high. Other dolls have their heads made from dental plastic and then covered with stockinette, and they have stuffed hands and feet. These are made in the schools and again every one is different, and with real hair. The children do not play with these dolls, they make them for sale as an exercise. Miss Gollmick told me that in all her travels out there she had never seen an Eastern child actually *play* with a doll. The band or sash above the waist is tied with a knot in front for a female, and left plain with the knot behind for a male.

Dolls from the Royal Harem of Kabul. Made of stuffed cotton fibre, and dressed in cotton, silk, velvet and damask. Made by the ladies of the Royal Harem in 1890. 12 in. high. Victoria and Albert Museum

Plan of legs

Elevation

Doll from Mirzapur, North West Provinces, India. Body of wire and stuffed rags coming down and dividing into two, acting as a stand with the feet showing in front of the skirt. This form of doll seems peculiar to these parts. Embroidered features. 1893. 10 in. high. Pitt Rivers Museum, Oxford

Dolls from the North West Provinces. The legs of the woman are stuffed, ending about 4 in. above the hem of her skirt. The man has very short arms. Embroidered features. Dressed in silks and silver tinsel.
Man 12 in. high, woman 10 in. high. Pitt Rivers Museum, Oxford

1. Doll from Bengal, made of stuffed cloth with stitched features. Blue tunic dress, edged with red, light-coloured trousers. 6½ in. high. Presented by Dr O. W. Sansom to the Horniman Museum. 2. Doll from the Shan states, Upper Burma. The merest bundle of cloth rolled up. Fawn colour. 3½ in. high. Presented by Dr O. W. Sansom to the Horniman Museum. 3. Wooden doll from Burma, jointed at the arms, and held by a wooden peg. 6½ in. high. Chelmsford Museum

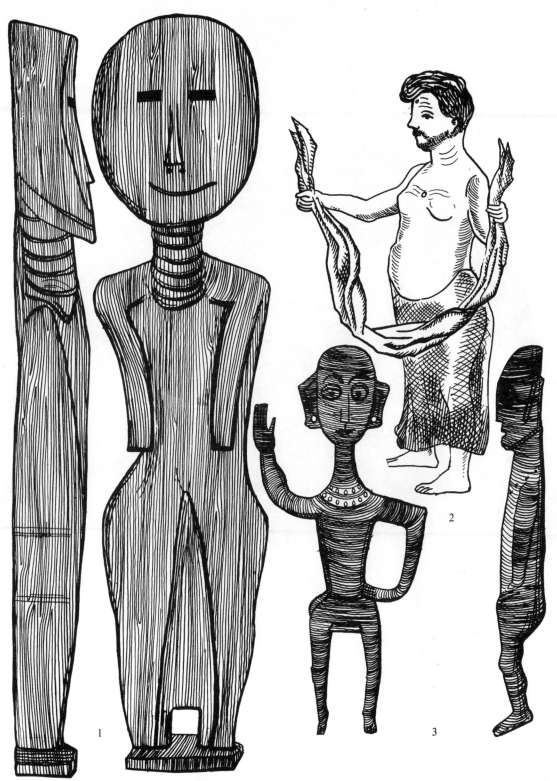

1. Doll for a boy. Eastern Angami, Kulazu, Bagwemi, Naga Hills. Carved wood with rings around the neck. Curiously like the spade-shape dolls of West Africa, but with different shaped body. 11 in. high. Pitt Rivers Museum, Oxford. 2. Man doll from Burma, carved wood. 6½ in. high. Chelmsford Museum. 3. Wooden doll from Konyak, Naga Hills, Assam, India. Very light to hold, with burnt features and pierced ears. 5¾ in. high.

Pitt Rivers Museum, Oxford

135

Chinese doll dressed as a mandarin. Composition with neck, head and hat in one piece. Hole between the thumb and fingers. From the Fleming Collection, but now belonging to the author. 10½ in. high

Chinese doll from the same collection. 9½ in. high

Paper models made by the Tonkinese and Annamese people, to be
burnt at funerals, for the use of the spirits of the departed. China

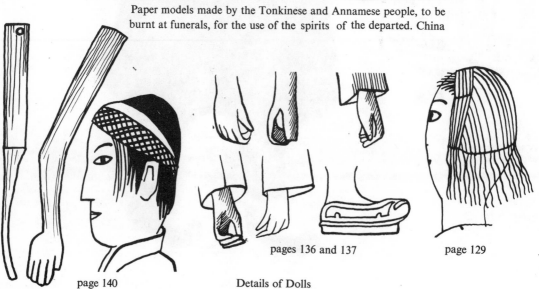

page 140

pages 136 and 137

page 129

Details of Dolls

Modern Chinese doll from Hong Kong, 1957. Composition with red finger-nails. Dressed in silk brocade, orange, yellow and green, with pink trousers, and shoes of the same material as the sleeves. Machine stitched. For sale in the Chinese shops. 10 in. high. Imperial Institute, London

Wooden boy doll from Korea, painted features, coarse muslin clothes. Fawn colour bound feet. 11 in. high
Pitt Rivers Museum, Oxford

Japanese doll with wagon and flowers. This is one of those dolls which are used at the Boys' Festival. It represents a strong boy of three years old, who once pulled a loaded cart up a steep hill. Embroidered robe of scarlet, with thick silk cord to the wooden cart loaded with a vase of artificial flowers. Doll about 15 in. high. Lent by the Prince of Wales, now the Duke of Windsor, to the Bethnal Green Museum

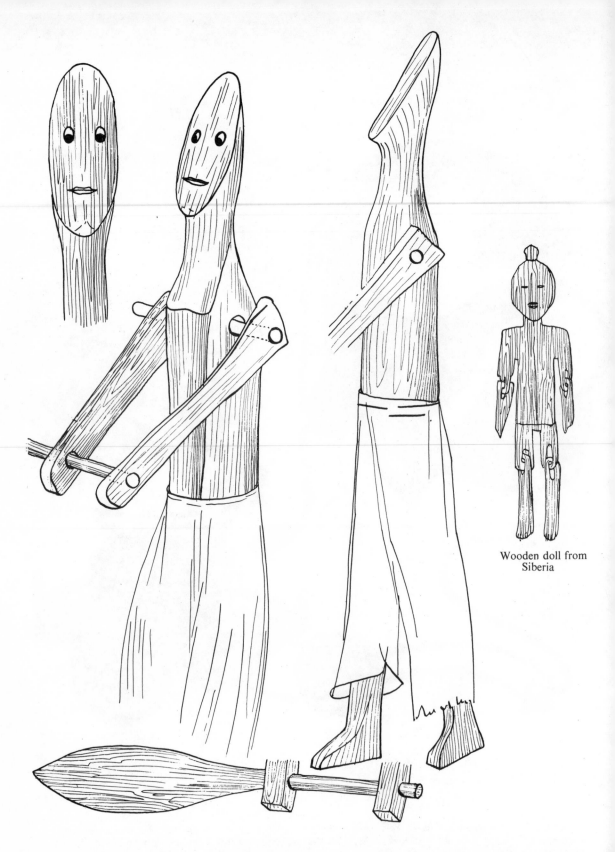

Wooden doll from Siberia

Wooden doll from Ostiak, west of Yenesei, Siberia. Movable arms and legs and holding a paddle. Simple cotton trousers, sewn with long stitches and with raw edge instead of hem. 16 in. high. Pitt Rivers Museum, Oxford

Side view of doll
from Malaya

Boy doll dressed in fibre cloak and apron, loose navy trousers, coat, white muslin vest, plaster hands and head,
painted hair and features, stuffed cotton legs. 9½ in. high. Horniman Museum

Modern doll from Malaya. Material, stuffed, face and arms of cream-coloured linen, stitched features, separate fingers. 8 in. high, 2½ in. head, again showing large head on a modern doll. Lent by Miss Sarah Clark

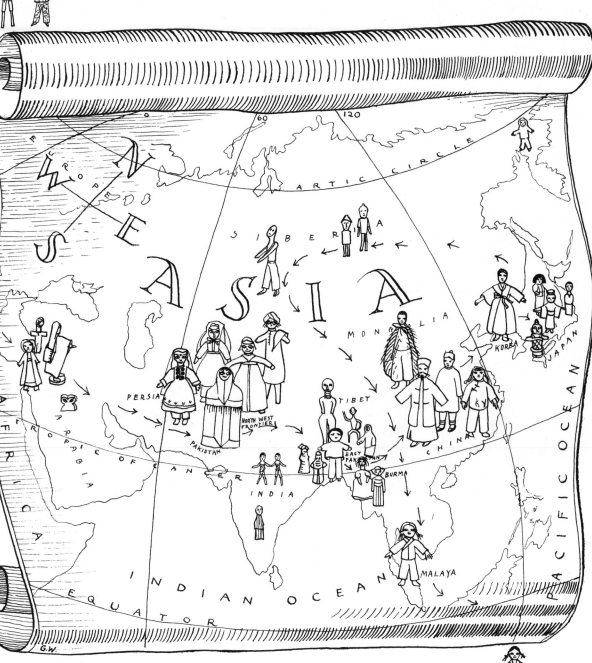

ASIA

In many parts of Western Asia dolls are not encouraged, as many superstitions exist, especially among the Mohammedan people, and yet we read that Mohammed himself was persuaded to play with dolls by his second wife, the nine-year-old Ayesha. There is a feeling among parents that a too realistic doll might come to life and do harm to the children, and some believe that a doll might even become a ghost. A girl from Persia, fearing evil from a doll, might place it for a while in a temple and thus decontaminate it, so that no harm would come from playing with it.

Actually many of the young children are employed in the making of carpets, so there is not much time for play, and even quite small girls are trained to carry weights on their heads so that they can fetch and carry water later on.

In Cyprus there are soapstone idols which are worshipped for promoting good harvests, and these take the place of the corn-dollies connected with harvests in parts of Europe.

In Palestine there are crude dolls made from forked sticks, with flat wooden discs for heads and the features indicated with ink. These are dressed in cotton cloth and sometimes have head-dresses of black net. Children also pretend with lumps of clay and pieces of wood, often leaving the face to the imagination, although, in Persia, we find quite realistic dolls with red fingernails.

1. A soap-stone idol from Cyprus

2. Doll from Palestine, made from a forked twig

3. Doll from Burma, to wear on the hand

4. Japanese substitute for a human sacrifice. Dressed as a warrior in armour. 6th century B.C.

5. Doll from Hyderabad, used in a smallpox epidemic. Wellcome Museum, London

The Arab people had dolls in the 6th century A.D., but many of the dolls among the Jewish children not only had no features, but no heads either.

Nowadays, the Arab refugees at the Refugee Camp Aqabatjaber, in Jericho, make dolls for sale, and the money goes towards their upkeep. Some of these are made on a wire frame, the hands looped around, and the dolls stand on wooden bases made by the boys in the camp. The heads and bodies are of material and stuffed, and the faces are made from fawn-coloured stockings. The features are worked with wool, black for eyes and eyebrows, red mouth, and two stitches at the nostrils, pulled fairly tight to simulate the nose. Real hair is sometimes attached, but their dresses are not made to come off. These dresses are authentic copies and may represent a particular figure.

Earlier dolls in Palestine, made from materials, often have very small heads, the proportion being about one-tenth of the length of the body. Features are stencilled on the canvas faces, which are left flat.

Dark-skinned dolls are also imported from Europe, and yet it is said by travellers that it is rare for them to see a child actually playing with a doll.

To make a cloth doll, a Persian girl will fold material over and over until it resembles a human shape, which she will then clothe in scraps of material and perhaps suggest features with paint. They also make dolls' houses containing many rooms, which may even be occupied by dolls from European countries, dressed in European clothes.

The horrible custom of laying the foundation of a building with a boy, often the eldest son, was altered by substituting an effigy instead, and this was one of the very good purposes to which a doll might be put. According to the Bible, when the town of Jericho was built by Hiel, the Bethelite, 'He laid the foundation thereof in Abrim, his firstborn, and set up the gates thereof in his youngest son Segub, according to the word of the Lord, which he spake by Joshua, the son of Nun.' All his children died during the process of building Jericho, which was probably about the year 1450 B.C.

* * *

Dolls play quite an important part in India, and often take the place of the hostess when a woman is forbidden to be present, and as gifts they are highly prized by members of Hindu households.

The Dassivah Festival of India lasts for nine days and at this time the girls place clay dolls in the river, and for three months they have no more dolls. These are substitute dolls, for the River Ganges used to have human sacrifices in the same way as the River Nile. At first the substitutes were life-size, but they gradually became smaller and smaller, until eventually dolls were used.

There are also the 'doctor-dolls' which are used in the countries where women must not be seen or touched by the physician. That part of the woman which needs attention will be pointed out or marked on the doll to indicate what is wrong with the patient. All the doctor will see is the doll, and he will prescribe treatment from looking at it.

Some Indian dolls are magnificently attired in velvets and gold and silver cloth, and may even ride upon splendid elephants whose tusks light up from inside by means of electric lights. There are two elaborate dolls, a Rajah and Ranee of India, in the Horniman Museum at Dulwich, just south of London.

Many of the stuffed dolls of India and Burma have embroidered features, and bodies made in the curious way of the doll I have drawn from Mirzapur, with the two 'feet' poking out, and others will be made simply as glove puppets. The hands and arms are tubes of material, stuffed like sausages, and the bodies and legs made in the same way, with perhaps wire inside to stiffen them. Much more care is lavished on dressing these dolls, which are trimmed with braids and embroideries, though nowadays some of the dolls are made more in the manner of those in Europe.

In India, dolls take part in the annual ceremonies which are held for girls before they are ready for marriage, and it is the custom to include dolls in the dowry of a bride.

At the Haldi-kunku gatherings which are sacred to the Hindu women, dolls are displayed, and there are other Indian festivals held throughout the year where toys and dolls are for sale and are given as presents to the children. Special days are set aside on which girls play with their dolls, these days almost becoming 'Dolls' Festivals'.

Wooden dolls similar to stump dolls represent various types of people; there will be peasants carved from a single wooden block to grand ladies ornamented with jewels. Soft cuddly dolls are made of stuffed material for the younger children, and costume dolls depict the various kinds of regional dresses just as in Europe, and are bought as souvenirs by tourists.

*　　　*　　　*

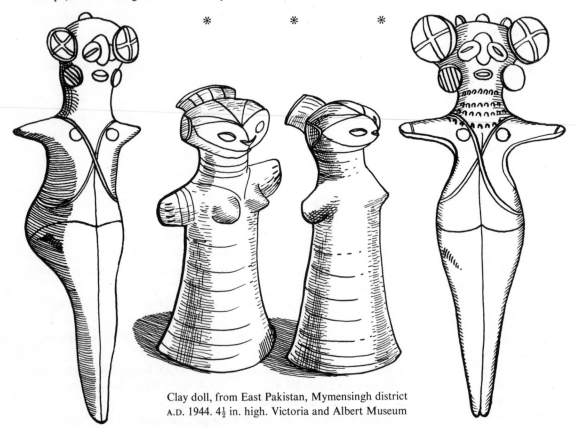

Clay doll, from East Pakistan, Mymensingh district
A.D. 1944. 4½ in. high. Victoria and Albert Museum

Terra-cotta Mother Goddess, North-west Frontier Province. 100 B.C. 6 in. high. British Museum

In Thailand, or Siam as it was called, the inhabitants build small houses near the entrance gate, and in these, spirits are believed to reside. These spirits are worshipped and cared for, and gifts of food and presents are placed before them every day at eleven o'clock, and incense is burnt. Among the gifts are miniature dolls and animals, and in this way the spirits bring good luck to the house and not evil. Every dwelling in Bangkok has one of these little spirit houses. Another custom here is that the children give presents on their birthdays instead of receiving them.

*   *   *

The history of the Chinese doll goes a long way back and dolls from these parts are well known, with their smooth faces and black almond-shaped eyes.

In the 5th century B.C. Confucius laid down a law that dolls must be used in the place of humans, for it had been the custom to bury servants along with their masters, and apart from this being very horrible, the population was gradually dwindling.

Here, also, religion sometimes prevents a woman from being treated by a male doctor, and again dolls are used. These Chinese 'doctor dolls' come in sets of twelve, each with a hand pointing to a different part of the body.

A woman will carry a doll on her back in the hope of becoming a mother, and it seems that this custom even happens in Europe as well as in Asia and Africa.

The Chinese children are taught at an early age that play is unprofitable to them, but in spite of this, many of the best dolls and toys came from this part of the world. Beautifully made and beautifully dressed, the Chinese dolls are well known and even the cheaper varieties are carefully made, with their pale yellow or white skins and inset shiny black slanting eyes and, of course, tiny hands and feet.

Small doll images were made of soapstone and talc, and amongst the Annamites in Indo-China straw dolls were used by the magic-men, and paper dolls used at funerals are burnt during the ceremonies.

Papier-mâché is used a great deal in the making of dolls. The heads and necks are usually in one piece and usually the little hands and feet are merely stuck in the armholes and trousers of the dolls and no upper arm or upper leg is used. They can sit about on small cane chairs in dolls' houses, and are not meant to be undressed.

Recently the drug heroin has been found concealed in the hollowed-out backs of Chinese dolls, these dolls being held by small children while they were carried through the customs by their parents.

*   *   *

Dolls in Korea are often made by the children from local materials. They take a bamboo stem, about five inches long, and in the top they put long grass to represent hair. This grass is salted and twisted, and then can be dressed to imitate the latest coiffure, and it is this 'hair' with which the girls love to play. Although the doll has no features added, perhaps a floury paste is used on the face, and the girls will spend much time arranging the hair with the aid of combs and hairpins.

A bamboo doll is often dressed in the clothes of a Korean woman and pushed about in a bamboo chair, and other dolls are made from straw and material stuffed. A Children's Festival is held on April 8th.

Modern dolls from Burma

The Burmese dolls have features worked in the same pattern as the Indian dolls. The diamond-shaped eyes seem a feature of these parts, and they are usually embroidered in black, with eyelashes on the upper lids. The higher the caste, the paler the face, and some dolls may even have white faces; the darker hued 'skins' are usually reserved for the servants and waiting men.

There are cheaper dolls also, with rag bodies and crude faces, and these are not so well made as those in China and Japan.

In Japan there are special Doll Festivals, the third day of the third month being the day on which the girls will hold their festival, while the fifth day of the fifth month is set apart for the boys. Weeks before these festivals, the shops will display their dolls, but no one may buy them until the great day itself arrives, and then new ones may be bought to add to an ever-growing collection. Every family of note will have accumulated dolls, some of which will be centuries old, the ancestral ones even having attained a religious significance, and the dolls representing royal personages will be especially valued. Although the actual feast lasts for one day only, the dolls will be exhibited for a week and then carefully put away for another year.

The girls' festival is known as Hinamatsuri and the boys' as Tango No Sekku, and the latter is celebrated by all families in which there is a son under seven years of age. Here, in the garden of the house in which the small boy lives, a tall pole is erected, from which a giant paper carp will float in the air.

The festival dolls are appreciated by the parents as well as by the children, and the dolls representing the Emperor and his wife have offerings of 'saké' made to them, this being the national alcoholic drink of Japan, which is made from fermented rice. The girls imitate the Japanese way of life with their dolls, but at the boys' festival their dolls represent warriors, some even on horseback, and heroes of popular tales. A platform is erected at both festivals and on these dolls are laid out with great care, the platforms being covered with bright cloths, red on the girls' day, and green for that of the boys.

Modern doll, from Japan

A Satsuma thread doll
in paper clothes

Japanese doll of about A.D. 1900, 4½ in. high. These could be bought in various sizes in English shops during the late 19th century, and early 20th, little ones costing only a penny. Lent by Miss Faith Eaton

Japanese doll-maker at work

Some with heads of plaster, others with heads of papier-mâché, all of these dolls will have pale yellow or pure white skins and slanting eyes with sweeping eyelashes, and eyebrows made with swift brush strokes. Their heads and necks are usually in one piece, or the head may fit over the neck, and the body may consist of the torso only, the lower arms and lower legs being attached to the clothes, thus enabling the dolls to assume sitting positions. The black hair on their heads is elaborately dressed in the traditional manner. A Japanese doll-maker will often arrange the clothes on a doll before fitting on the head.

The dolls are gaily dressed in rich silks and much embroidery, depending whom they are representing, as the royal dolls will be extra grand. The horses, carts, utensils and the little things used at these festivals are all beautifully made from wood, papier-mâché, and silken threads, and decorated with typical Japanese designs.

Of course, the children play with dolls all the year round, and these can be bought in the shops in the usual way. The small ones, about 4 inches high, could be bought for a penny at the beginning of the 19th century in England, but these have disappeared from the shops and are more likely to be found in collectors' cabinets nowadays. In Japan, today, there are dolls made from composition, and rag dolls made over a wooden foundation and dressed in the traditional manner.

Scapegoat dolls used to be given to mothers in order to ward off evil, and these were set up on the banks of streams, and in some parts the custom still persists. The dolls were crudely made, as they were not meant to last, and were often just a shaved willow stick with hair on top which was made of shavings, and the dolls were dressed in paper clothes. These dolls were supposed to take on the sins or the illness of their owners.

Another doll, used for much the same idea, is made by the Japanese children with a rounded clay base. This doll is sometimes made near a temple and then taken home and placed on a 'god-shelf'. The face is made of paper and there are two white discs where the eyes should be. Prayers are said to the doll, and being rather like a 'tumbler doll' it rises to a vertical position, the quicker, the better. The doll is promised eyes if the prayers are answered, and should this happen, two black dots will be painted in the centres of the two white discs.

There are other tilting toys in Japan, one being known as the 'Posti', that is, addicted to opium; others may represent an old man, and be made of paper. Some say this represents a figure of Buddha, others that it is Daruma the Buddhist priest who sat for nine years on a rock without moving. In Japan these tilting toys are known as Ot-tok-i, that is, the Erect-Standing-Ones, and they are usually made of paper, with the weighted base filled with clay. There are others made representing a woman riding on a tiger, and although these tumbler dolls are found all over the world in various disguises, they may have originated here.

As birthdays have already been mentioned, it is interesting that children but no grown-ups celebrate their birthdays in this part of the world, and that the New Year is the collective birthday for all adults.

✳ ✳ ✳

In the Malay archipelago there are dolls which are made from Chinese copper coins, and with faces of coloured sandalwood. These are dressed in coloured cloth, the favourite colours being red and white. Modern dolls from here are made of material and stuffed; they have features of stitched wool, woollen hair and their hands are carefully made with the fingers separated. These, also, are often dressed in printed cottons, again red and white predominating.

In 1850, gutta-percha was exported from here to Europe for the making of dolls' bodies.

✳ ✳ ✳

Manchuria has dolls carved in bone, and in Siberia there are dolls made from pinewood, some of these having very clever link-like joints and rather large flat faces. The Ostiaks dress their dolls in cotton material and little woolly caps, and in the north are dolls made from the teeth of the walrus, where wood is difficult to obtain. There are also dolls made from fur scraps, and it is interesting to remember here the dolls which came from Alaska, the point from where we first started.

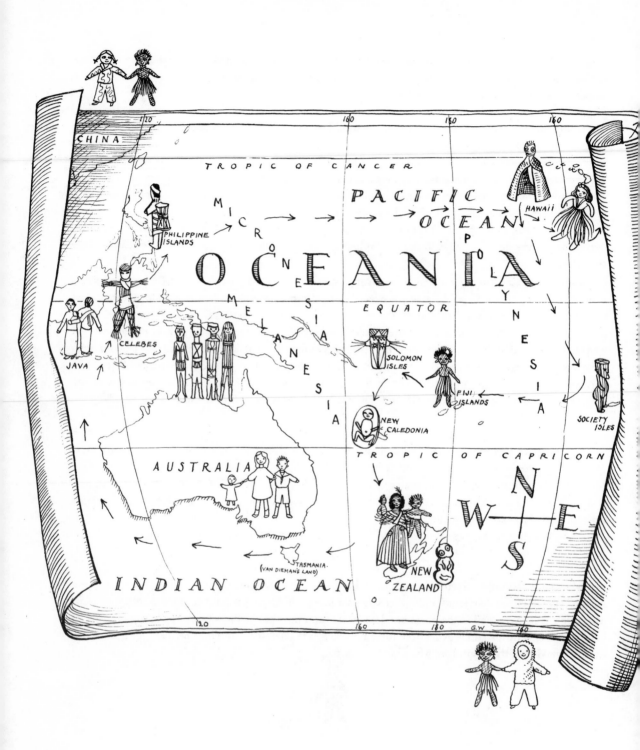

CHINA

TROPIC OF CANCER

PACIFIC OCEAN

MICRONESIA

OCEANIA

PHILIPPINE ISLANDS

Hawaii

MELANESIA

EQUATOR

CELEBES

SOLOMON ISLES

JAVA

FIJI ISLANDS

POLYNESIA

NEW CALEDONIA

SOCIETY ISLES

TROPIC OF CAPRICORN

AUSTRALIA

N
W E
S

TASMANIA
(VAN DIEMAN'S LAND)

NEW ZEALAND

INDIAN OCEAN

DOLLS OF OCEANIA

In New Zealand many of the early dolls were carved from nephrite; bones and stones being used as implements. The dolls were used as amulets and were believed to be a protection for the mother as well as for the child against evil spirits, and sometimes these dolls would be passed on to the child as a plaything. The New Zealand aborigines have few children and little girls may marry when they are only eleven years old.

Some natives here, and elsewhere on the Australian islands, keep small carved wooden figures in their homes for the ancestor spirit to live in, but these are not playthings, and prayers are offered to them and also to those figures representing the god Tangarva. The wooden image of this god is hollow, and smaller wooden images are put inside as offerings. These must not be confused with dolls, as they have no play significance.

Many of the native dolls of New Zealand wear a curious green-stone ornament on a thread around their necks. This is made by the Maori people, and is valued highly. It may be formed in the shape of the human foetus, some having a semblance of carved ribs, but what this ornament really represents seems to be lost in obscurity. It is more of a charm than an ornament and may be a kind of fertility symbol. It is known as the Pounamu. There are several of these charms in the Wellcome Museum, London, and in the British Museum there are many of different sizes, some of them being far too large to wear as ornaments.

Among the Melanesians there are wooden figures with tattoo marks, the hair and beards being made from heads of corn and the lozenge-shaped eyes made from mother-of-pearl.

The New Zealand Pounamu

Australian child wearing a forked twig

On the island of New Caledonia the women have a birth amulet which is peculiar to these parts. This is a wooden doll, lying in a wooden cradle or tray, and spread out fairly flat. The woman will buy one of these amulets if she and her husband desire to have a child. She gets it from a medicine-man, and she takes it home, rolls it up in her mat, and goes to sleep with it. When her wish has been granted, she keeps the doll hung up on the walls of her hut, presumably as a protection against evil for herself and her child, in the same manner as other primitive people.

The Fiji Islands have dark-skinned dolls, with raffia skirts and sharks' teeth necklaces, wearing bright flowers in their hair. On the Santa Cruz Islands, curious designs are painted on wood, some pieces of wood being about 4 inches long, and having a semblance of a nose and two eyes. On the Lepers' Island, people amuse themselves with cat's cradles, which seems to be a pastime for many primitive people in other parts of the world, and has significance other than that of amusement.

Children play with all kinds of toys on the Solomon Islands, and here are bottle-shaped dolls with ornaments and real hair. A male spirit doll, known as Menata, takes care of the health of the women, and a woman on the Torres Straits will carry a male doll if she wishes to give birth to a boy.

✳   ✳   ✳

There are few native dolls from Australia, and it seems that children use their imaginations in their play, making do with stones and sticks rather than with actual dolls. A few wooden figures were introduced into the northern part of Australia by the traders from Malaya and Macassar.

These traders travelled down the coast in search of pearls, tortoiseshell, manganese, sandalwood and timber, and they taught the natives how to carve the wood. The 'milkwood' of the Leichhardt fig tree, being soft, was easy to carve with a knife or spear, and the figures were always carved from the round and not from planks, the circumference of them being oval in shape. The whole figure would be smeared with red ochre and then incised into patterns. This Tolemic painting plays an important part, and as the figures became sacred, they were not used as playthings.

The Australoids wear no clothes and really do not need to make anything. The little girls pretend to cook, and the small boys play at hunting, and the less primitive ones build shelters or 'wurlies'.

When the children play at fathers and mothers, they either use their smaller brothers and sisters instead of dolls, or they will use stones or wood, and even flowers and leaves. Like other children, they look after the good ones and flog the naughty ones, and these things can all be left behind when the family decides to move on to another place.

Children are trained to carry babies by using a forked stick, which is placed across the back of the neck, in the same way that other people use a carved doll. They are quite content to leave the forked stick or 'lawyer cane' just as it is, making no attempt at carving a head, arms or legs, and of course no clothes, as they wear none themselves. By the lower Tulley River, these sticks are called 'kuckara' and the forked ends dangle over the shoulders of the child, which is good practice for when she will carry a real baby. If the right kind of stick is found, knees can be imagined.

In Queensland, children will carry their dolls in little bags known as 'dilly-bags', and the same idea is used at Cape Bedford. In South Queensland the children seem quite content with forked sticks, but some figures resembling women are made from gum cement, and are probably used as dolls. Others pretend with pieces of wrapped bark, which they stuff with grass.

A story I heard when at Australia House is worth repeating. Some native women were given dolls for their children, but the children never received them. Apparently the mothers thought that while they kept and guarded the dolls, their children too would be kept safe from harm.

Another story I heard was of some aborigine women who were out with their children. Suddenly they came across a little girl who was nursing a life-like doll. They were quite perturbed, thinking that she was mourning over a dead baby, so they joined her and 'mourned' over it as well.

In the bigger towns and villages of Australia, there are dolls as we know them in England, and the Australian children will play with these just as other children do, and the same applies to New Zealand, and in all other parts where white people have made their homes.

About 1843, a native woman of Van Diemen's Land, Tasmania, was seen to be carefully arranging several small stones on the ground. These were about 2 inches wide, flat and oval, and they were marked in several directions with black and red lines. She said that these stones represented absent friends, and that one stone which was larger than the rest stood for a fat native woman on Flinders Island, who was known as Mother Brown.

✳   ✳   ✳

Java is well known for its puppets and shadow figures, but the dolls also wear masks in the same way as the natives do in their dances.

In New Guinea, boys and girls play at cat's cradles, using their toes as well as their hands, but amongst the Mafula people the children have no dolls or toys and amuse themselves by running down grassy slopes and playing at tug-of-war.

Doll masks, from Java. About 2¼ in. high. British Museum

Wood carving from Trobriad Island and Toy canoe with three leaf sails

The Dyak people are fond of their children, but do not have many toys with which to play. Usually four in a family, the women seem to pound rice all the day long, though some of the girls play with roughly carved wooden dolls, and the boys spin tops and make boats. The wooden images of Borneo are supposed to bring luck to the people, and these are made from wood which is often gathered from some remote place, sometimes by moonlight. The Dyak women have little houses filled with dolls, which they believe will avert illness for expectant mothers.

The Bataks of Sumatra carry dolls for fertility reasons, and these are shaped rather like jars, with heads of brown wood, sometimes covered with tin. Some hang lucky images in their houses over their money chests in the hope of bringing luck to the hunters or of increasing their wealth. There is the little figure of a wooden man hanging over the 'Poor-chest' in St Alban's Cathedral, in Hertfordshire, England, so perhaps he is there to bring the poor people luck and also to increase their wealth.

The girls and women on Keppel Island nurse dolls in their arms like real babies, and these are made in the shape of cones. They vary in length up to 15 inches and are coloured with red ochre. Named 'Kamma' after the grass tree, they are intended as charms for begetting fine children, just as are the flat wooden dolls of West Africa.

1. Fiji Islands, dark-skinned doll from Suva wearing a straw skirt, flowers, earrings and a necklace of sharks' teeth
7 in. high
2. Hawaiian Islands; the whole doll is made over a jaw-bone foundation, with terra-cotta-coloured cloth and ends of string. 5½ in. high. British Museum
3. Society Islands, not a toy but a little wooden figure. 1 ft. high. British Museum

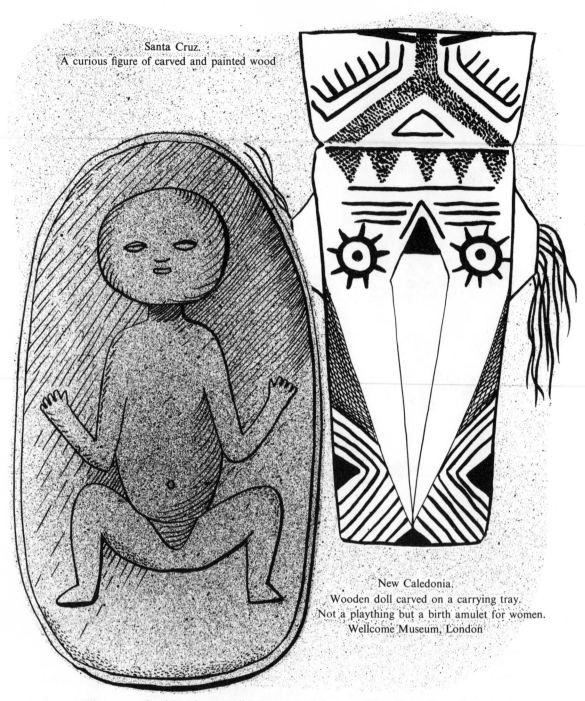

Santa Cruz.
A curious figure of carved and painted wood

New Caledonia.
Wooden doll carved on a carrying tray.
Not a plaything but a birth amulet for women.
Wellcome Museum, London

When a couple wish to have a child, the woman buys one of these from the medicine man

See opposite page

Maori doll from New Zealand. Stuffed linen, flat face, arms stitched to sides of body. Skirt of hollow grasses, black enamel stripes. Hessian cloak trimmed with hens' feathers. 13 in. high. Lent by Mrs Nerea de Clifford

*DOLLS*LANDING*IN*AUSTRALIA*

A Gopi board from New Guinea. When it is used as a house amulet, the string from which it is hung allows it to turn in any direction from which a sickness is expected. It can also be hung in the bow of a canoe to bring good luck in fishing and to keep the fishers safe

Dutch East Indies. Man doll of brown fibre, bound with raffia cut in strips

163

Philippines. Doll of coarse cloth, stuffed, hand-stitched features, cloth hair, woven braid dress, beautiful little basket 1½ in. high. Doll 5 in. high. Lent by Miss Julia Russell

Java. Modern doll of carved wood, very light, weighing less than 2 oz. 6½ in. high. Lent by Miss Juliet Russell

Honolulu. Dolls wearing straw skirts, boleros, beads and flowers

Madame Montanari's Dolls at the Great Exhibition of 1851, class 29, case 122. In the North Transept Gallery. From William Clark's book on the Crystal Palace, issued at that time in penny parts.

DOLL COLLECTING

In studying dolls, one is amazed to realize what a great deal of time, thought and money must have gone towards the manufacture of these playthings for children – and I should add for grown-ups, because the model and fashion dolls were made for them.

Young children have dolls with which to play, perhaps a favourite to take to bed, another to push in a pram, or carry in a carry-cot, just as real babies are carried in cars today, so a lucky child gradually accumulates quite a doll family and, in a way, becomes a doll collector.

As children grow up, the dressing of dolls becomes more important than actually playing with them. Later, the dolls are only brought out now and again, or might even be passed on to some younger relation. In this way, a doll becomes gradually older than her dress, especially if she has been handed down and redressed many times.

Sometimes an older girl begins a collection of dolls, more as mementoes than as playthings, the collection growing and her knowledge of costume growing with it. It is strange that many of these dolls will wear grown-up costume rather than that of children, which is exactly what happened to dolls previous to 1855, when the first baby dolls were made in France.

A doll collector could collect dolls from various countries, especially if in the habit of travelling, or the collection could be limited to one continent, and the various items of history pertaining to that part of the world. Who, for instance, would have thought that dolls could be made from the scraps left over from celluloid collars?

'The oldest dolls' would indeed make a strange collection, 'large dolls', life size, would make another one, and 'the smallest dolls in the world' yet another. 'The most well made' would include those made by famous doll-makers, and would become an expensive hobby, as the value of some of the playthings of the past is gradually increasing. The long-ago plaything in the attic has become a part of history, and if the date be known, or maybe the period when the doll was played with, then she will be most interesting, especially her dress and the little garments underneath.

Early dolls often have earlier dates put on them to make the doll appear more valuable, whereas dolls which owners have possessed when children are often given later dates to make the owners appear younger.

The actual craze of collecting dolls is not recent; they were even collected in the 17th century. But Doll Clubs belong to the 20th century, about 1930, and today there are a number in America, and some in England under the name of the Doll Club of Great Britain. The president, Mrs Graham Greene, has a valuable collection of dolls and doll's houses. Dolls and doll collecting are discussed in these clubs, and the important business of organizing exhibitions of dolls in aid of charity. There are men members as well as women, which is not really strange, for after all, the top fashion designers are mostly men, and one of our most famous architects, Sir Edwin Lutyens, designed the doll's house which was built and equipped as a present to Queen Mary. It can be seen in a special room at Windsor Castle, together with many dolls.

Many private collections eventually find their way into a museum or country house open to the public, and some of these devote a room or old nursery to yesterday's playthings. Lydia, Duchess of Bedford, speaking at a Doll Exhibition in aid of the Blind, mentioned that she put dolls in some of the rooms of Woburn Abbey, in order to give them a more occupied appearance, and in the Van Cortlandt House Museum, New York, dolls sit about on chairs in the nursery.

The first half of this book has dealt with what could be termed the folk dolls of the world, and the slight geographical background will be of interest to the collector, who, while gathering together these dolls, may ponder on how they came to be. Those much travelled people, the stewardesses of air liners, bring dolls back as mementoes, and Samuel Pryor, Vice-President of Pan American Airways and a well-known collector of world dolls, suggests that if there are people on Mars, 'You can be sure that there are Martian dolls'.

However, many collectors specialize. Some may limit their interest to the 'Queen Anne' type doll with her countrified face and wooden body, whereas others may concentrate on demure fashion dolls of wax or smiling baby dolls for a child.

China, Bisque, Parian, Rubber and Celluloid are only a few headings under which dolls might be grouped. Pedlar dolls are a speciality in themselves and could really be classed as ornaments, for their silver 'toys' and minute wares were guarded by glass domes while residing on a plush-covered table in the parlour rather than in the attic nursery.

The United Federation of Dolls' Clubs, U.S.A., issues a magazine entitled *Doll News* which comes out four times a year; at present in England we have a news sheet called *Plangon*.

Doll collectors who belong to clubs often meet in one another's houses, where makers' marks are discussed and animated conversations take place on weighted eyes, swivel necks and mortise and tenon joints. Some members learn how to mend their dolls, others make wigs, and at the Brooklyn Children's Museum, New York, there is a doll club at which girls learn to make dolls and also their costumes.

However, at all these meetings dolls are present, and maybe they smilingly keep to themselves some secret item where the unwary collector has gone astray.

Lady Maria Arnold, 6½ in. high, carrying a hemmed handkerchief marked with red initials M.A, dressed by the Baroness Lehzen

Mlle Proche, 6 in. high, dressed by Queen Victoria

A few of Queen Victoria's own dolls, from the London Museum, Kensington Palac

Two children of Mrs Dudley, 2 in. and 3¾ in. high

Mlle Constance Lecomte, 6½ in. high,
married to Prince Alexis Poniatowsky,
dressed by Queen Victoria

ese little dolls were all dressed between 1831 and 1833

Jointed wooden doll with inset marble-like blue eyes, painted head and shoulders, arms stitched to dress and jointed at elbows. Dressed in canvas dress worked all over with embroidery with flowers, leaves, and looped fringe edges. Bonnet, cape collar, two front panniers, looped fringe at hem. 21 in. high. Geffrye Museum, Shoreditch

Heavy wooden jointed doll, coated with gesso and painted. Stuffed upper arms, hair sewn to canvas, enamel eyes glued in wooden grooves. Dressed in white with red lines, white woven socks with red tops, black beads. 27 in. high. Geffrye Museum, Shoreditch

Doll in summer dress, about 1850. Sprigged white muslin dress over glazed cotton petticoat, short muslin jacket, straw hat. Glazed china head and shoulders, kid arms, separate stitched fingers, pink kid body and legs, no joints, no toes. Dress hooks at back with same fulness all round, long muslin knickers edged with pink and lace, long white cotton socks, black shoes with velvet strip across toes, black soles, no heels. 14 in. high. London Museum

SIMONNE

Doll by Simonne of Paris. Cream kid, bisque head and shoulders, painted eyebrows, inset eyes, wig fixed to canvas on kid. Bisque arms, hands, pink nails, kid scalloped where joined over bisque. Kid legs, four stitched toes, gussets at knee, two slight breasts and body like a Jumeau. Long white drawers, chemise, shaped and boned corsets, flannel petticoat, and white frilled petticoat. 14 in. high, marked No. 1883. London Museum

173

Doll representing the Princess of Wales in her wedding-dress. Married in 1863, she later became Queen Alexandra. White bisque head, brown wig, wooden hands. Brown canvas body with cream shiny wooden legs, black painted boots, brown soles, no heels. White silk taffeta dress trimmed with net, silver wire and orange blossom. White satin ribbon sash. $9\frac{1}{4}$ in. high. London Museum

Dolls' Heads – 1. Wooden doll with inset glass eyes, pierced ears, hair stitched to canvas glued to head, wooden hands with separate fingers. Head 3½ in. high. Given by the Misses Rickman to Hove Museum.
2. White glazed china doll (porcelain) with black shiny hair. 1868. Head 2 in. high.
Given by Mrs Rankin to the same museum
3. White glazed china doll with black hair (porcelain), dark brown leather hands. Head 2¼ in. high. Early Victorian.
Given by Mrs Cooper to the same museum, near Brighton

Early 18th Century Wooden dolls, 'Queen Anne'.

DOLL DETAILS

The head of a doll is a most interesting feature, and luckily a head often remains intact when the body of the doll has almost perished. The proportion of head to body varies with the period to which the doll belongs, and heads have gradually become larger, until in some dolls they are too big in scale for the rest of the body.

Necks and shoulders vary with current fashions; long or short necks, wide or sloping shoulders, all contribute towards dating a doll, and many dolls suffer from having the arms joined to the body too low down, which gives a loose appearance to the whole figure.

Details like lips, nostrils, eyebrows and ears, all give a clue to the period at which the doll was made, apart from more obvious items such as eyes and hair.

Until recently, bodies have not had much care devoted to them, except in baby dolls, but now grown-up dolls have shapely parts, and care taken in the modelling even where it will be covered by clothing.

Hands have often been made too small; they should be the length of the face from the chin to the hair on the forehead, in a well-proportioned doll, and the size of a foot should equal the length of the head. These proportions vary with the age the doll is meant to represent, as children have larger heads in proportion to their bodies, but, there again, a doll may have its proportions altered to suit the fashion of the day, or what is considered to be beautiful in its home country.

Legs depend on whether a doll is meant to stand up on her own, and there have been numbers of dolls with no legs at all. The Victorian dolls had such small feet that only the stiffness of their gowns or crinolines or paper bustles enabled them to stand erect.

The early wooden dolls have their heads carved, with painted features and perhaps a little human hair gummed on. Later they have inserted blown-glass eyes or enamel ones, and the ways in which eyelashes and

English doll of
painted wood
1730

Head of Meissen China
marked with crossed
swords 1880

Victoria & Albert Museum

eyebrows are indicated are most interesting and various. Queen Anne, Georgian, Victorian and Edwardian were all periods in which wooden dolls were made; these include the 'Dutch' dolls, and other kinds from the Continent. Of the Peg-dolls, and Penny-woods, the little dolls dressed by Queen Victoria and her governess have become famous. These have 'spoon'-shaped hands, and often a high yellow comb at the back of their small wooden heads. They have been referred to as 'common twopenny Dutch dolls' and are from about 3 to 9 inches high. Beautifully dressed and decorated with beads and shaded ribbons, white knitted socks made by the Baroness Lehzen, they were dressed by her and Queen Victoria between 1831 and 1833, and they were all packed away four years before Victoria's accession to the throne in 1837. However, the four eldest Princesses were fond of playing with dolls, so they may often have been taken out of their strong wooden chest, and the little hats and hemmed handkerchiefs admired.

Dolls with moulded papier-mâché heads, made about 1820, are very beautiful. Later they were mass produced by the Wolverhampton firm of Evans and Cartwright, often being made in a dozen different sizes. By 1840, many of the papier-mâché heads had wax-coated faces, the features being painted on the wax, but later, about 1855, the features were painted on the papier-mâché faces and then coated with a clear tough wax, giving a most delicate finish to these heads. Hair wigs were made from goats' hair, rather than from human hair.

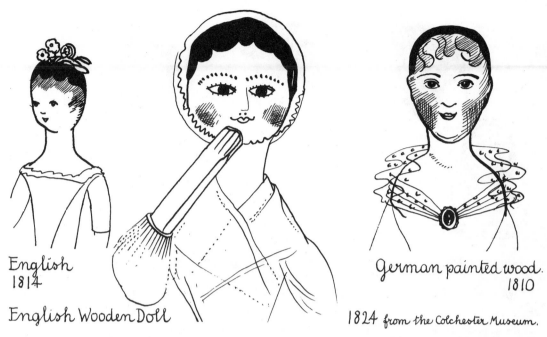

English
1814

English Wooden Doll

German painted wood.
1810

1824 from the Colchester Museum.

Very beautiful dolls, but more fragile than those of wood, are the wax kind, and it is surprising that so many of these have survived to the present day. They are easily broken, the wax-coated faces can chip, and the solid heads can melt. Many of these dolls are fashion dolls, some made by the Montanari family or the Pierottis, the former being noted for the beautiful dresses in which they clothed these waxen dolls. The child-like faces and the pinky skins of the Pierotti baby dolls are easily distinguished, and when dressed they wear long clothes and veils, as was the custom in Victorian and Edwardian days. The fashion dolls look their best on stands, as these display their dresses to advantage, for they were never intended as playthings, but all of these wax dolls must be well cared for, and kept away from heat and bright lights.

Many of the fashion dolls, in their day, were kept under glass domes, in the manner of clocks and stuffed birds, so careful were their owners of the dresses and the hair-do's. One of these is in the museum at Truro in Cornwall, and here, also, is a miniature room containing gentlemen and lady dolls sitting in a drawing room in after-dinner fashion. The men have white glazed china heads, and the ladies real hair carefully arranged, in contrast to the highly glazed black shiny hair of the menfolk.

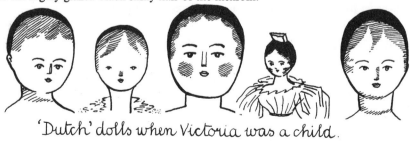

'Dutch' dolls when Victoria was a child.

Goodyear Rubber, 1839. Composition, 1845. Porcelain, 1831. Composition, 1845. Rubber 1839.

There are many varieties of china dolls, highly glazed or with a matt surface. Porcelain, bisque, stone china, bone china, all are used for the making of dolls' heads, sometimes the head and shoulders, and also for the hands and feet. The potteries of Europe made many more than were made in England, there being a great demand for dolls' heads as they were stronger than the kind made in wax and those of papier-mâché.

When the head and shoulders formed one piece, a hole was made at the front and back, in order to join it to the stuffed body, and later two holes were made in the front and two at the back, this being a stronger method than the previous one.

Earthenware figures were made from the 17th century onwards, and the word porcelain still denotes white earthenware in Holland and in Scandinavia. In the mid 1740's, English figures were made in soft porcelain, and those in hard porcelain were made about 1768. True porcelain was patented by William Cookworthy of Plymouth in 1768, and that which was made from a marble-like paste was known as parian-porcelain. This is usually pure white, but it can be slightly off-white also.

Soft-paste porcelain was known as biscuit in 1771, and during the second half of the 18th century, all *unglazed* pottery and porcelain was known as biscuit. There was soft biscuit and hard-paste biscuit, the soft ware being porous and difficult to clean.

Figures of bone-china were made in 1800, and parian ones in 1842, and many of the porcelain dolls' heads came from Coburg and Sonneberg. Germany exported many china heads, some of these coming from factories at Dresden.

In 1846, Copelands of Stoke-on-Trent introduced parian porcelain, and the sharpness of modelling made the biscuit figures appear more like marble. Between 1855 and 1870, dolls were made from parian and in 1862 there were some of tinted unglazed biscuit porcelain.

Spode, in 1805, made what we in England call stone china. It was a northern product of Europe, hard, impervious to liquids and salt-glazed. Figures were at first hand modelled, but later they were moulded. John Astbury made figures, not dolls, in salt-glazed stone-ware.

Glazed China 1850, English doll with wig, 1859, German Papier Mâché.

In the 18th century all kinds of white pottery were known as china, but in the 19th century the name china was given to translucent porcelain, and in the 20th to English bone porcelain. China clay is the English equivalent for kaolin.

In England, the word bisque or biscuit is applied to unglazed pottery, feeling almost like a biscuit when touched, but in the doll world, an ordinary china doll is known as a bisque, and a glazed one as porcelain. In America, the white dolls' heads are known as parian, and the cream-coloured ones as stone-glazed.

The tiny arms and legs were made, often, in a different factory from that of the heads, and were then assembled in yet another place, so it is no wonder that heads and limbs are sometimes of different scale. The body was long compared with the head, perhaps to make the doll appear larger, and the feet and hands tiny in proportion to the complete doll. Some china legs were made with socks to the knees, or with button boots or shoes, the china legs being dipped in the various glazes, and brown or yellow soles added later.

Complete dolls and dolls' heads were made at the Crescent Potteries at Stoke-on-Trent, until the outbreak of war in 1939. These were made of parian, complete in various sizes, and in both black and white. The 'white' dolls and the 'black' kind were sometimes marked with the name 'Corona', but these dolls are no longer being produced, and the Crescent Potteries function no more.

Porcelain boy. Truro Museum. Jenny Lind, 1852. Glazed China, 1860

1860 1866 Helston Museum 1860

Pedlar dolls were fashionable in the late 18th century, the very early ones having metal toys on their trays and some wearing quilted petticoats. In 1830 some were dressed as market women; many of these had no legs and some just a wooden stump.

Mechanical, musical, walking, speaking and swimming dolls are not nearly so recent as one would suppose, and it is amazing what ingenuity went to their manufacture, and how well the mechanism works, even when the doll has lain idle for several years or even for a whole century.

One of the most beautifully dressed baby dolls, with all the accessories, can be seen at the Bethnal Green Museum, London. This English doll has a Dutch layette of 1895, prepared by Mrs Twiss, of Hilversum, in 1899, for the International Exhibition at Amsterdam. The doll, known as Princess Daisy, was presented to the Duchess of York, later Queen Mary, for the infant Princess. The layette consists of six embroidered robes, a cot, feeding utensils, jewellery and much other equipment fit for a miniature princess. Amongst the jewellery, contained in separate cases of pale blue velvet, is a silver rattle, gold bracelet, 'Daisy' brooch and a real pearl necklace with a diamond clasp. This doll, with all these things, is lent to the museum by the Princess Royal.

The museum at Luton, Bedfordshire, also has many beautifully dressed baby dolls wearing long clothes, apart from the well-known straw dolls of that locality.

Papier Mâché head, painted & dipped in wax, fair ochre hair, inset ultramarine eyes.
Doll belonging to Miss Blair Hickman.

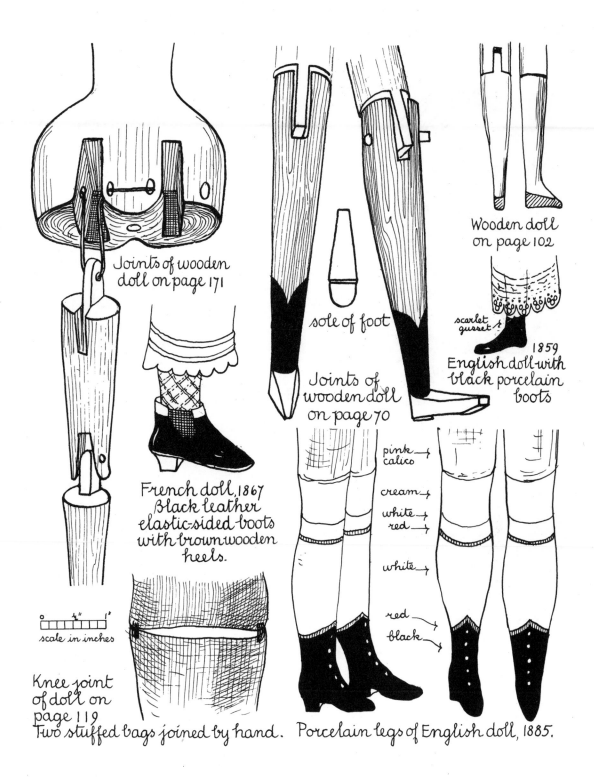

Joints of wooden
doll on page 171

Wooden doll
on page 102

sole of foot

scarlet
gusset

1859
English doll with
black porcelain
boots

Joints of
wooden doll
on page 70

French doll, 1867
Black leather
elastic-sided boots
with brown wooden
heels.

pink
calico →

cream →

white →
red →

white →

red →

black →

0   ½"   1"
scale in inches

Knee joint
of doll on
page 119
Two stuffed bags joined by hand.   Porcelain legs of English doll, 1885.

183

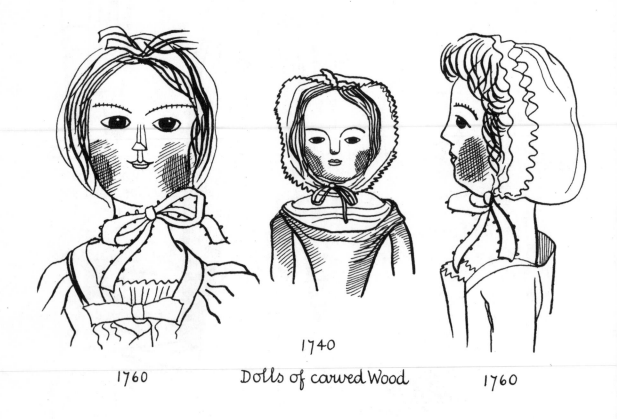

1740

1760   Dolls of carved Wood   1760

DOLLS' HAIR

In England, during the 18th century, a fee was charged to view the dolls displaying the newest hair styles, and often a doll or a doll's head was made expressly for this purpose, and would have a most elaborate hair arrangement, sometimes quite exaggerated.

Ringlets standing away from the head were the fashion during the 17th century, and a doll had this style imitated by the use of wire. Later, various materials were tried, easier to manage than human hair, which needed a great deal of preparation. Thread, string, wool, silk, animal's hair, such as that from the horse, cow, sheep and goat, and even paper, have all been used for this purpose and today there is a very silky substitute for hair, made of nylon.

Frequently, a doll of the 17th or 18th century would have a little hair fixed to the head with gum, with the ends poking from beneath a muslin cap which was never removed. Others had hair stitched to coarse canvas which was then glued to the wooden head, and was usually brown and straight.

painted

1828
Wooden doll, painted rather yellow, painted eyes, and with brown moulded hair. The limbs have ball joints. Dress is of brown silk.
In the Victoria and Albert Museum

Wax dolls have hair arranged in various ways, and even when the hairs were inserted with hot needles, they could be put in singly or in small groups. Sometimes the groups were arranged in spiral form, finishing at the 'crown' of the head, in a natural manner; others were inset to emulate a particular hair style, and would be arranged with a centre or a side parting, and often with a fringe, depending on the fashion. A number of doll-makers at this time made beautiful wax heads into which hairs were inserted. The Montanari dolls exhibited at the Crystal Palace Exhibition of 1851, which were made of wax, with inset hair, had long flowing locks, sometimes falling well below the waist. Miss Blair Hickman has a Montanari doll with hair about 14 inches long in her well-known collection.

The circular plaits fashionable during the early part of Queen Victoria's reign were arranged on the dolls to be seen from all angles, and the hair styles were carefully copied on the china dolls also.

There were special workshops for the making of dolls' wigs, and although the dolls' dresses were often made in the homes, the wigs were more often made in factories, and these were usually fixed to the heads before joining to the rest of the body. Sometimes the hair was sewn, strand by strand, usually very straight, and with a centre parting, and even quite small dolls would have hair done in this way, which would be a simple matter compared to the complicated pictures which were made at this time with human hairs.

A wax doll with wig of fair hair, 1855. Luton Museum

A bisque head by Bru, with eyes to open & shut. 1890

A wax Montanari doll with inset hairs

In the middle of the 19th century in France a doll's wig cost anything from 2 francs 25 centimes to 15 francs for a dozen of them at wholesale price, but the dolls with inserted hairs were more expensive. In 1849 the Parisian dolls had curled and dressed hair; and in 1855 Mr Voit of Hildburghausen exhibited dolls whose heads were of cardboard, and 'the hair dressed with taste'.

China dolls of 1840 had black glazed hair imitating corkscrew curls, and a waved effect with a central parting appeared in 1855.

About 1850, dolls' hair was often made from silk; this was an improvement on the flax and astrakhan, which proved to be too knotty. The silk hair took the place of the hair of moulded 'cardboard'. Artificial flowers adorned the heads in 1860, and china heads and wooden ones had flowers gummed on the top.

Simple hair styles became complicated until, in 1878, dolls' hair fashions were imitating false hair additions, huge plaits sometimes stuffed and padded, and ringlets here and there.

Although red hair was popular about 1879, there were few dolls with this colour, though the proportion would be about the same as among humans with natural red hair. An auburn-headed doll, with a 'bun' at the back of her head, is in the Victoria and Albert Museum, but china-headed dolls had black hair, and dolls with fair hair were usually the bisque variety.

The French fashion was to brush the hair forward from the back of the head and mass it on top during 1880 and by 1900 the hair was waved, fluffed out at the sides and turned back over a 'Pompadour' pad.

Male dolls had black china hair, highly glazed, and lady dolls dressed for parties wore ribbons and bunches of curls at the back and sides, known as 'Greek chignons'.

If a doll had her hair washed, it was curled again with curling tongs, which were heated on a methylated spirit lamp. Generally a mother would undertake this job, as the cooling of the tongs on pieces of paper was a dangerous pastime.

During the 1914–18 War, many a child was in trouble for 'bobbing' the locks of her doll, for bobbed hair was now the fashion, and it was some while before dolls could be bought with this hair-do.

Permanent waving came about 1920, and most dolls had curly hair, fair being more popular in England than dark; the dark-haired dolls were more in demand abroad.

A doll of today usually follows the fashion of children's hair styles, and can have short hair, long hair with plaits and bows or a pony-tail effect, which looks well and is in keeping with the dungarees and duffle-coats which a modern doll might wear. The curls are permanent, the hair washable, and many dolls are provided with their own shampoos.

1850

Porcelain head and shoulders from West Europe. Tinted cheeks and red top to eye lid.

1840

Porcelain head & shoulders from West Europe. Tinted cheeks but no red line over eye lid. Brown comb at back.

1865

English Porcelain with tinted cheeks and red top lid. Two holes back & front.

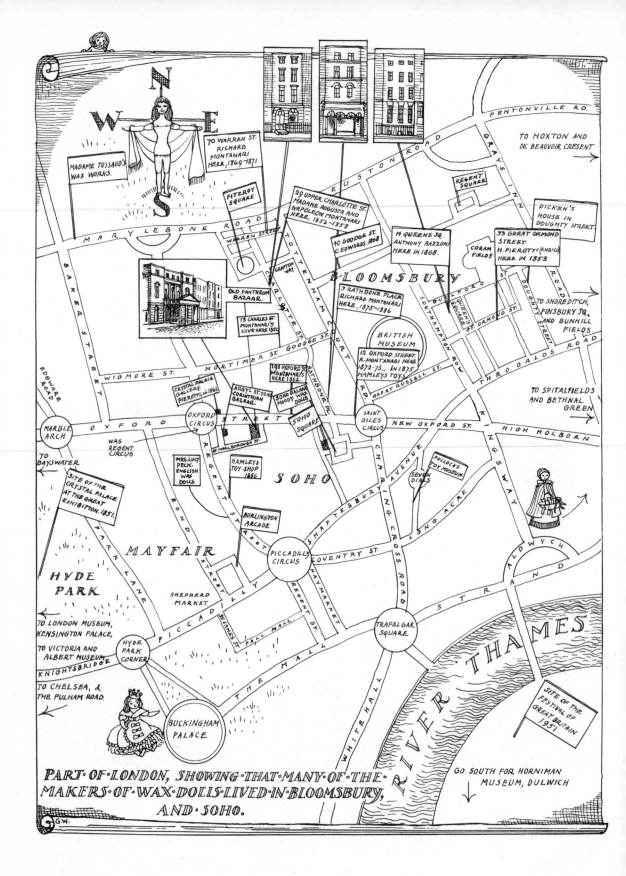

MADAME TUSSAUD'S
WAX WORKS.

70 WARREN ST.
RICHARD
MONTANARI
HERE, 1869~1871

FITZROY
SQUARE

29 UPPER CHARLOTTE ST.
MADAME AUGUSTA AND
NAPOLEON MONTANARI
HERE, 1852~1858

REGENT
SQUARE

TO HOXTON AND
DE BEAUVOIR CRESENT

PENTONVILLE RD.

DICKEN'S
HOUSE IN
DOUGHTY STREET

40 GOODGE ST.
C. EDWARDS. 1868

14 QUEENS SQ.
ANTHONY BAZZONI
HERE IN 1868.

CORAM
FIELDS

33 GREAT ORMOND
STREET.
H. PIEROTTI (ENRICO
HERE IN 1853

MARYLEBONE   ROAD

WARREN STREET

GRAFTON WAY

BLOOMSBURY

OLD PANTHEON
BAZAAR.

3 RATHBONE PLACE
RICHARD MONTANARI
HERE, 1875~1886

TO SHOREDITCH,
FINSBURY SQ.
AND BUNHILL
FIELDS

13 CHARLES ST.
MONTANARI'S
LIVE HERE 1850

BRITISH
MUSEUM

12 OXFORD STREET.
R. MONTANARI HERE
1872~73. IN 1875
HAMLEYS TOYS

WIGMORE ST.

MORTIMER ST.

GOODGE ST.

THEOBALDS   ROAD

TO SPITALFIELDS
AND BETHNAL
GREEN

CRYSTAL PALACE
GALLERY.
PIEROTTI, IN 1861

198 OXFORD ST.
MONTANARI'S
HERE 1862.

ARGYL ST. SOHO
CORINTHIAN
BAZAAR.

SOHO BAZAAR
MOODY. WAX
DOLLS

OXFORD
CIRCUS

STREET

SOHO
SQUARE

SAINT
GILES
CIRCUS

NEW OXFORD ST.

HIGH HOLBORN

MARBLE
ARCH

OXFORD

WAS
REGENT
CIRCUS

ST. MARLBOROUGH ST.

TO BAYSWATER

SITE OF THE
CRYSTAL PALACE
AT THE GREAT
EXHIBITION. 1851.

MRS. LUCY
PECK.
ENGLISH
WAX
DOLLS

HAMLEYS
TOY SHOP
1886

SOHO

POLLOCKS
TOY MUSEUM

SEVEN
DIALS

BURLINGTON
ARCADE

MAYFAIR

HYDE
PARK

SHEPHERD
MARKET.

PICCADILLY
CIRCUS

COVENTRY ST.

BOND   STREET

TO LONDON MUSEUM,
KENSINGTON PALACE,

TO VICTORIA AND
ALBERT MUSEUM

KNIGHTSBRIDGE

TO CHELSEA, &
THE FULHAM ROAD.

HYDE
PARK
CORNER

PICCADILLY

PARK   LANE

ST. JAMES ST.

PALL MALL

REGENT ST.

HAYMARKET

TRAFALGAR
SQUARE

RIVER   THAMES

BUCKINGHAM
PALACE

THE   MALL

WHITEHALL

SITE OF THE
FESTIVAL OF
GREAT BRITAIN
1951

GO SOUTH FOR HORNIMAN
MUSEUM, DULWICH

PART·OF·LONDON, SHOWING·THAT·MANY·OF·THE·
MAKERS·OF·WAX·DOLLS·LIVED·IN·BLOOMSBURY,
AND·SOHO.

G.W.

DOLL-MAKERS OF THE 19TH AND 20TH CENTURIES

The London makers of English wax dolls lived fairly close together in the districts of Soho and Bloomsbury, and a few of the actual houses in which they lived are still there today, although the bazaars in which many of them sold their goods have long since disappeared.

One of the oldest of these London bazaars was the Pantheon in Oxford Street. This was opened in 1772 as an opera house, but it was burnt down and rebuilt in 1795. Domenico Pierotti exhibited his wax dolls here as early as 1793. It occupied a large Soho site on the south side of Oxford Street. It had three entrances; one at 359 Oxford Street, another at 40 Poland Street, which runs at right angles to Oxford Street, and the third entrance facing south at 8 Marlborough Street. The facade was imposing, with well-placed windows on three stories and a fine portico with four columns making an arcade over the Oxford Street pavement. Inside was a theatre and a public promenade, so there would be plenty of people visiting the bazaar and viewing the dolls and other things for sale, and in 1834 it was a well-known place. However, it was closed down in 1867, and Gilbeys, the wine merchants, took it over, lending the southern portion of it as a temporary church.

Another old bazaar in Oxford Street was Queen's, but this was burnt down in May 1829, together with the Diorama.

The Soho Bazaar was opened by a Mr Trotter in 1816, to relieve the relatives of persons killed in the Napoleonic War, the Battle of Waterloo having been fought the previous summer. This bazaar was near the Pantheon, being a short walk eastwards towards Soho Square, where it occupied numbers 4 to 7, and also numbers 6 to 9 in Dean Street. It was at this bazaar that, later on, E. Moody displayed the wax dolls made by Charles Marsh. Incidentally, Queen Victoria always insisted on reviewing her own troops, and small girls would take their dolls, which were dressed to represent the Queen, on these occasions, holding up their dolls to see the soldiers.

In 1858, the London Crystal Palace Bazaar was opened in Oxford Street near Regent Circus, now Oxford Circus. The corner shop on the north side was No. 112, and next door but one, at No. 108, was a shop known as the Gallery, London Crystal Palace, and it was here that Enrico Pierotti had his wax dolls. In 1861, this Pierotti was awarded a bronze medal for his Royal Model Dolls. The site of this bazaar is now occupied by the firm of Peter Robinson, which has spread gradually from the corner shop.

Not far away, across the road, almost opposite the Gallery, is Argyll Street, and here at No. 7, the Corinthian Bazaar was opened in 1867 to replace the Pantheon Bazaar which had closed that year. Argyll Street runs southwards from Oxford Street to Great Marlborough Street, and on the east side this bazaar was built where Argyll House stood. Today the site is occupied by the London Palladium. This bazaar remained open for only a year, and was closed again in 1868, but during this time, Charles Marsh exhibited his wax dolls here.

The wax-doll maker, Antoni Bazzoni, lived at High Holborn in 1852, but later he moved to 14 Queen Square. This was a particularly large house, with four floors and a big basement below ground level, and facing the gardens. Often, at this time, it was the custom for craft-workers to share a large house and work in it. Perhaps this house was such a one; it is still there, and close to a large hospital.

Near by, in Great Ormond Street, No. 33 was the home of the Pierotti family. This is a row of typical town houses; many are still there, but unfortunately No. 33 has been pulled down and the Paris Laundry now occupies the site where lived this famous family of wax-doll makers.

Beyond the Pierottis' home and eastwards across the Gray's Inn Road is a small turning known as Constitution Road, and here in 1853 lived J. Barton, another maker of wax dolls. The house where Charles Dickens lived is on the way, and here may be seen some tiny dolls representing characters from Dickens stories, and made entirely in paper.

Madame Montanari seems to have moved a great many times during the thirty-five years or so when she made her dolls in the Bloomsbury district. Napoleon, her husband, started in Regent Street, and later she lived in Upper Charlotte Street, on the left-hand side approaching Fitzroy Square. Later they moved to Charles Street, between Mortimer Street and Goodge Street. The building of the Middlesex Hospital, founded in 1745, and gradually enlarged, probably accounted for one of their moves, as Charles Street has now disappeared and the entire site is occupied by the hospital.

Strange that this family of wax-doll makers also lived so near a hospital. Perhaps Napoleon Montanari worked there, as from time to time the services of a clever wax modeller would be required in the hospital. Many of the medical models were beautifully done in wax, being lifelike with natural colouring. Some even had curled human hair, inset eyelashes and eyebrows, and it was difficult to tell the models from the real thing. Maybe Napoleon modelled some of these and that it was from him that Augusta learned to make dolls with such care. Napoleon's life-size wax effigy of a figure in the last stages of consumption must surely have been made in a hospital, and when exhibited at the Crystal Palace, it would have brought him many commissions.

Plastic has now taken the place of wax for medical models, just as it has also done in the manufacture of dolls, not only the playthings, but for life-size dolls which are used as models by nurses when studying child welfare and the care of babies. Nylon threads inserted into the vinyl heads replace the human and animal hair used on the wax models and the heads of wax dolls, these plastic figures being far stronger than those of wax.

Later, the Montanaris moved into Oxford Street, but their son Richard went slightly northwards, passing the house in Charlotte Street, across Fitzroy Square, to 70 Warren Street. This was a smaller house, but soon he moved to No. 12 Oxford Street, a few doors away from St Giles Circus. Later this shop was occupied by Hamley's Toy Shop, and Richard went to No. 3 Rathbone Place near by. This is a small turning on the north side of Oxford Street, and was a good site with a beautiful shop front. However, he shared this building with other people, and fortunately No. 3 is one of the few remaining houses in Rathbone Place which was built in 1778.

Other makers of wax dolls also lived in the Bloomsbury district. Goodge Street and Great Russell Street both contained doll-makers, and it is quite likely that many of them were acquainted one with another.

Across the river, on the southern side of the Thames, John Edwards made dolls of wax and composition, and H. J. Meech, doll-maker to the Royal Family, also lived in this direction.

By 1894, Charles Marsh moved to the Fulham Road in South Kensington. This beautiful little house is still intact, with its lovely wooden shop front, two sash windows above, and two higher 'dummy' windows.

The present owner told me that it may be pulled down in the near future, which seems a great pity.

114 Fulham Road, London S.W. Sketched in February 1960
One time occupied by Charles Marsh, Wax doll maker.

The makers of wooden dolls seem to live in a more easterly direction of London, that is in the districts of Clerkenwell, Hoxton, Houndsditch and Bethnal Green. Spitalfields, too, is in this area. On the way are Bunhill Row and Finsbury Square, in which makers of wooden dolls lived and worked. Composition dolls and rubber dolls also come from the east, and on either side of the river. Like the wax dolls, these wooden dolls were sold in the bazaars, markets and shops, or they would be carried from door to door by pedlars.

M. JUMEAU AND SON

The first mention of Monsieur Jumeau, doll-maker, which I have found, was at the Industries Fair in Paris, the year 1844, when he and Monsieur Belton showed 'naked and dressed dolls'.

At this time they lived in the rue Salle-au-Comte, and won Honourable Mentions. Here is their entry:

M. M. Belton et Jumeau, à Paris, rue Salle-au-Comte 14
Ont exposé une collection soignée de poupées nues ou habillées qui sont très-bien fabriquées: ils en font un grand commerce dont une partie pour l'exportation.

Monsieur Jumeau and his son made dolls between 1844 and 1898, which became well known for their large eyes. The dolls were of bisque, though some of the early heads were of German make. The ones with the large eyes were their own, and the early ones have shut mouths.

Their first dolls had bisque heads and busts or, rather, shoulders, and these were fitted onto the bodies of kid, though later on the arms and legs would also be of bisque and their heads fitted to more chubby bodies, but even the late 19th-century dolls still had the extra large soulful eyes.

The pale cream or white and sometimes pink bodies of the kid dolls had arms and legs, also of kid, with gussets at the elbows, hips and knees, to allow for bending. On the large dolls, often fashion dolls, the fingers were separated carefully and stuffed, but on the smaller dolls, they were stitched to show the divisions.

The Jumeau family took a great deal of trouble with the dresses and underclothes of the dolls, and at the Crystal Palace Exhibition of 1851, they sent over some dolls which were awarded a prize medal for the Dolls' Dresses, which consisted 'of the outer robes together with the under garments'.

The report of the jury on their exhibit is as follows:

1851. P. Jumeau. Paris, Prize Medal for Dolls' Dresses. The dolls on which these models are displayed present no point worthy of commendation, but the dresses themselves are very beautiful productions. Not only are the outer robes accurate representations of the prevailing fashions in ladies' dresses, but the undergarments are also, in many cases, complete facsimiles of those articles of wearing apparel. They might serve as excellent patterns for children to imitate and thus acquire the use of the needle, with a knowledge of the arrangement of colours and material: in the latter respects they might indeed afford valuable instruction to adults.

The Jumeaux kept up the reputation they had won at this exhibition, and when they showed their baby dolls, the famous BEBES JUMEAU, at another exhibition in 1855, they again attracted attention, and it was remarked that 'they were elegant and in good taste'. These dolls were of blond bisque, the colouring being applied and fired in.

In 1858, again, the bisque dolls won prizes. This time there were several kinds, the best ones being labelled 'La poupée de luxe'.

Amongst wax dolls, jointed necks are rare, and as far as I know, the Jumeau family never made one, but the son did invent a movable neck for a bisque doll, and in 1860 they patented the swivel neck. I think it was the son who invented this idea.

By 1862, the Jumeau dolls were quite famous; their well-modelled heads, waxen complexions, life-like eyes and movable joints attracted much attention. The baby dolls had the eyelashes and eyebrows carefully painted, and the wig hair was fixed onto canvas and cork. There was a 'ball-joint' at the elbow and at the knee, but no movement at the wrist and no teeth. The ears were carefully modelled and were to scale with the head, the top of the ears being particularly pronounced.

By 1880, most of their dolls had these ball-joints, and in 1890 they made a Talking Doll, in which was concealed, in the chest, a phonograph with five changeable records, which enabled the conversation to be altered.

Between 1892 and 1900, there was an Elie Jumeau, a sculptor, of Paris, who amongst other things made plaques, at first in France and later on at Cheapside, London.

An early fashion doll made by Jumeau would be about 16¾ to 17 inches high, with the head 2¾ inches high and with the body about 6½ inches long. The china head with swivel neck, I should say bisque, was a pale pink flesh colour with deeper pink cheeks, pink nostrils and mouth, with the shoulders merging into the cream kid body. The eyes were of a deep blue, large and with white lines and black pupils. The doll would have pale fawn painted eyebrows in sweeping lines and painted eyelashes. The wig of nut-brown hair, made with a centre parting, fell to the waist.

The kid body was made on a wire foundation and was made to fit very smoothly over the bisque shoulder piece. The arms and legs had gussets at elbows, thighs and knees, separate fingers and stitched toes, and the ears would be pierced for earrings. On the back, at the waist, would be the mark Jumeau, Medaille d'or, Paris, showing that he was awarded a gold medal for his dolls.

A later Jumeau 'baby' doll of about 24 inches high would again be marked on the back in the same manner, and would have ball joints at elbows and knees, but no joint at the wrist. The wig hair was fixed to cork, the eyes still very large and the eyebrows again painted with sweeping strokes and painted eyelashes. The ears were pierced, even on some of these dolls, and the rather flat ears were to scale with a pronounced line at the top. A 24-inch doll would be marked size 10, with a small X at the side, and the smaller size dolls would be marked with a higher number.

The details of the Jumeau baby doll, which I made at Miss Blair Hickman's, are of the doll described as the highlight of the 1959 Exhibition of Dolls held at the Ceylon Tea Centre, London, in aid of the Blind. She was photographed in the arms of Lydia, Duchess of Bedford, who opened the exhibition.

The Jumeau factory, at Montreuil, in France, employed both men and women in the making of dolls.

These dolls were made in fourteen sizes, the largest being 3 feet 3 inches high. The early models had their heads and busts in one piece. These were moulded and made from porcelain clay and were later joined to the bodies which were made in heavy steel matrices, the hollow parts being stuffed with paper damped with paste. The bodies had narrow waists, fashionable at this time, and each limb was made in a separate mould, but in the same manner, a more complicated machine being used for the hands.

When all the body parts were dry, the women glued hollow balls to the extremities of the limbs. A ball was fixed to each shoulder corresponding to the upper part of the humerus bone in the human body, and another ball fixed to the top of each leg, where the femur fits into the pelvis. Each limb of the doll was provided with a ball and a hook, the thigh bone being set into the groin. These hooks were already bent and cut by a boy employed for this purpose, and the arms, legs and bodies were assembled and joined together with copper wires.

Next, the grey pulpy bodies and the limbs were ready for painting. Layer upon layer of salmon-pink paint was applied, each layer being allowed to dry before the next was added.

Whistles were put in some of the bodies, and the eldest son of the Jumeau firm invented a movable neck.

The position of the eyes was found and cut out, ready to have glass eyes inserted from the back of the hollow face. These eyes were glued firmly in place and did not move. Many firms imported the glass eyes, but the Jumeau ones were made in the same factory, usually by women. This was a skilled job, involving the use of white glass rods, which were heated and the end formed into a round marble, which was gradually shaped into an almond, by pulling at the corners. A rod of coloured glass was also melted and put inside the white rod before the marble was formed, and as each marble was tapped off, another could be made, and so on. If movable eyes were needed, the upper part of the eyeball would be painted a flesh colour to represent the lid, so that when the doll was laid down its eyes would close by means of a counterbalance, and this method was used for a number of years.

The bold sweeping strokes of the eyelashes were painted by women, as also were the eyebrows, and the wigs of human hair or that of the Tibetan goat were made in another part of the factory. The hair was stitched to muslin or canvas, imitating a 'parting', and this was fixed to small cloth skull-caps by small nails. The hollow porcelain heads were filled with cork, before having the skull-caps adjusted. Usually the hair was fixed to the head of the doll before this, in turn, was joined to the body.

The dolls were attired in dresses, and socks and shoes fitted to their feet. Often the shoes of red-brown leather were decorated with ribbons, cockades, rosettes or buttons. Others wore kid boots, pumps or dancing slippers, which were sometimes white or red. Many wore very large hats trimmed with feathers, and their silk dresses and rustling petticoats gave a very rich effect to the attire of these French dolls.

MONSIEUR BRU

He was another maker of French bisque dolls, and his had rather thickly painted eyebrows and parted lips. The ears were small, the necks fairly wide and the eyes made to open and shut. The faces on his dolls were rather fat and square.

In 1849, he invented an internal organ which permitted the body of the doll to move backward, forward and sideways. This doll was made of kid with a groove in the upper leg.

Bru seems to have been keen on mechanical things. He made a doll in 1867, in which the head turned showing two expressions, and in 1869 he took out a patent for perfecting the manufacture of dolls. In 1872 Madame Bru made a 'magical talking doll' which sang various airs, so altogether they contributed greatly to the world of mechanical dolls. Casimir Bru, junior, patented a feeding doll in Germany in 1879.

In 1880, the head of a Bru doll seemed to have its face heavier and more highly coloured. Some were made of kid and others of wood, and these would have no joint at the waist.

In 1898, Monsieur Bru and Monsieur Jumeau together formed 'La Société Francaise de Fabrication des Bébés et Jouets,' and in 1899 this society had a capital of 3,800,000 francs.

A Bru doll will sometimes be marked with his name on the shoulder.

Casimer Bru.   Feeding doll
                page 226.

THE PIEROTTI FAMILY

The dolls which were made by this family are very beautiful with most lifelike skins of wax, the waxen parts of the dolls being made in moulds.

These moulds were in pieces and tied together. The hot wax was then poured into the moulds so that the head and bust would be in one piece when the mould was untied. The slight roughening on the wax which would come at the edges of the mould would then be smoothed down. Similarly the arms and legs would each be made from a mould, normally in two sections, so that when the mould was untied, each arm or leg would be in one piece. These parts were hollow, the wax being of a fairly even thickness throughout.

The wax on the Pierotti dolls was coloured by a secret process before being moulded, the pinker dolls having a touch of carmine in them, and others being the exact colour of flesh. The cheeks were tinted, the corners of the eyes reddened, also the nostrils and the ears and of course the mouth. The arms and legs were left the same colour throughout.

Many drawings must have been made before the moulds were constructed, as the dolls have natural curves, the necks especially being most realistic. The baby dolls have a very natural thickening of the fold of skin at the back of the neck and in the dolls where the head was slightly turned towards its left shoulder, the creases in the neck were faithfully modelled. At the wrists are two folds and small creases are at the ankles, and the little hands have their nails indicated, dimples marked near the knuckles, and the small feet also had nails on the well-modelled toes, and again dimples.

The actual body of the doll was made of ordinary strong white calico, something almost unknown today, and stuffed with cow hair.

The seams are at the doll's sides and the legs have a seam on the inside edge and likewise the arms. The body itself is shaped with a smallish waist and with wide hips, and where the legs are joined on is a line of stitching, quite flat, in order that the doll could be put in a sitting position.

At the lower edge of the shoulder piece are two holes in front, and two holes at the back, these holes being bored with a hot needle or spatula when the wax had cooled, and finished off with brass eyelets. Two similar holes were made at the top of each arm, and also at the top of each leg and eyelets inserted. The waxen parts of the doll were then joined to the torso by threading double white threads through the holes and stitching them through to the canvas in fairly large stitches.

As the wax parts of the dolls are hollow, they are not unduly heavy to hold. The glass eyes were inset and fixed with blobs of wax on the inside, great care being taken to make the two eyes focus correctly. These eyes would be either of a clear colour or of the paper-weight variety and may have been imported. Thin eyelashes were embedded into the wax on both top and bottom lids and sometimes the eyebrows were of real hair and sometimes they were indicated with painted lines. In the dolls which I saw at Miss Muriel Pierotti's, the eyes were fixed and the lids did not open or close.

The hair on the dolls is most interesting, being carefully inserted in small groups by cutting into the wax with a sharp knife. The use of a sharp knife for inserting the hairs is emphatic, as the widow of C. E. Pierotti states that she has never seen hot needles used for this work. Starting at the perimeter of the head and gradually circling round until the crown was reached, each little group got nearer and nearer together towards the centre of the head, the groups starting at about a distance of $\frac{1}{8}$ inch apart and with fewer hairs near the forehead and ears. Some dolls had flaxen hair and others a nut-brown; the hair also may have been imported, and a great deal of refining was done before using.

The Pierotti dolls do not seem to be marked with a signature, though there may be a slight mark under the shoulder piece. If a doll should get broken it could be sent back to be mended, as these dolls were definitely meant for children to play with, and they have beautiful faces with happy expressions. The ones I saw had their lips closed with a smile, and I saw none with teeth showing.

A typical doll of about 1900 would be made of white calico and hollow wax. With a length of 20 inches, the head would be about 3 inches high, with brown eyes and black pupils, brown hair, and a beautiful pinky wax 'skin', coloured with carmine, giving a distinctly alive appearance. The brass eyelets are threaded with double cord joining the waxen parts to the stuffed body.

Another Pierotti doll of the same period would be 22 inches long, with head and shoulders $4\frac{3}{4}$ inches high, again with lovely pale pink skin, inset fair hair, and blue eyes with deeper blue rims to the iris.

A smaller size would be 10 inches high, with head $1\frac{3}{4}$ inches high and shoulders $2\frac{3}{4}$ inches high and $2\frac{1}{2}$ inches wide at the base, all again carefully modelled and joined to the stuffed body. Even the dolls of only $6\frac{1}{2}$ inches long have cloth bodies, but on these the wax limbs are glued instead of being stitched.

Apart from the dolls made for children, the Pierottis also made grown-up models and busts in wax, many from drawings made from life.

The first known doll-maker in this family was Domenico, who came to England as a boy in 1780 and began making dolls in about 1783. It is said that John, son of Marie Tussaud, went to one of the Pierottis in order to learn their method of inserting hairs into wax, but there is no proof of this. Yet another made dolls for the English Royal Family, one being commissioned to make dolls to place on the wedding cake of one of the Royal Dukes, this being the custom at that time in England, Denmark, Germany and elsewhere.

In the 1851 Exhibition there was a G. Pierotti of Austria, a decorator who showed a painted library, and another one, Giuseppe Pierotti, a sculptor of Milan, who showed a group of Carrara marble entitled 'Cupid's Vintage'. I have yet to discover if these were any relation to the doll-makers.

Henry was a wax doll-maker in 1854, and the family supplied Hamley's, now in Regent Street, with dolls until about 1930. In 1861, a Pierotti was styled Inventor of the Royal Model Dolls, and in 1862 Henry Pierotti was awarded a bronze medal at the International Exhibition. Giving his address as 13 Mortimer Street, Oxford Street, Henry exhibited Wax Model Dolls with inserted hair, together with other wax dolls and figures, and Celia, his daughter, showed foreign and English toys.

Great care went into the making of each doll, and anything not quite perfect would be cast aside. The large dolls would cost about £5 in 1900, and the smaller ones approximately 25s. There is a typical Pierotti doll in the Geffrye Museum at Shoreditch.

The Montanari and Pierotti families, all doll-makers, lived fairly close to one another for a number of years and it is certain that they knew of each other. Miss A. M. Pierotti tells me that

My father distinctly recalled a Montanari calling to see his father. He described him as a very tall, strikingly handsome man from South America: he thought he was an actor, but did not know of him as a doll-maker. My father was then only a child but his memory was exceptional.

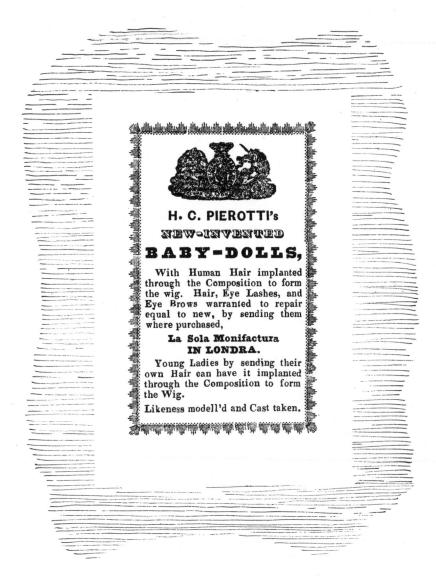

H. C. PIEROTTI's

NEW-INVENTED

BABY-DOLLS,

With Human Hair implanted through the Composition to form the wig. Hair, Eye Lashes, and Eye Brows warranted to repair equal to new, by sending them where purchased,

La Sola Monifactura
IN LONDRA.

Young Ladies by sending their own Hair can have it implanted through the Composition to form the Wig.

Likeness modell'd and Cast taken.

THE MONTANARIS

This family of wax modellers came over to England during the second half of the 19th century and established themselves in London, where they soon settled down to earn their living doing wax modelling and specializing in dolls' heads.

In 1836, in Paris, lived a family of the name of Montanari, who were mostly doctors of medicine, there being one, Louis, who wrote a treatise on the treatment of dysentery. I wonder if there is any connection between this family of doctors and the Napoleon Montanari who later modelled in wax an anatomical specimen, portraying the last hour of life in 'consumption'. This figure was modelled from nature, and was shown in 1851 at the Great Exhibition, when he was living at 29 Upper Charlotte Street, Fitzroy Square, fairly near to some of the large hospitals.

Montanari is not an uncommon name, and at the same exhibition, one Alessandro, a decorator from Milan, showed the vaulted ceiling of a library. He may have been no relation, but it is difficult to say whether the 'Doll' Montanaris came from Italy, France or South America, before they settled in England.

They were a skilful family and were entrusted with much delicate work, gradually building up a reputation for their life-like dolls with their beautiful workmanship. Soon they became famous, and their work was known abroad as well as in England. Great care was taken with the expressions on the dolls' faces, and by the time they were taken out of the moulds and finished off, no two looked exactly alike. Some of the dolls have a slightly open mouth, and some have a faint droop at the corners, giving their owners somewhat sad expressions, which have been described as demure.

Great care was taken with the hair, though the Montanaris were by no means the only doll-makers to insert the hairs singly into the wax by means of hot needles. Where the hair met the forehead and cheeks, a natural look was achieved by arranging the hairs farther apart, and the eyelashes and eyebrows were also copied faithfully from nature and each hair inserted separately. As the wax heads were hollow at the neck and shoulders, they would be held in the hand or propped up on stands while the hairs were being inserted and then pressed into place.

The head, neck and shoulders were all in one piece so that there were no swivel necks. The hollow wax arms came to just above the elbow, and the legs to just above the knee, and the hands and feet were carefully modelled from life, with dimples on the backs of the hands and two creases at wrists and elbows. The faces were rather round, the necks short and fat, and the shoulders fairly wide and sloping so that they looked well in low-cut dresses. The waxen parts of the dolls were joined to stuffed bodies made of glazed chintz or calico, usually white. The heights varied; some dolls were small, others about 25 to 27 inches high, and others larger still. The large dolls, when they were not dressed, were sold for about 5 guineas in 1851.

Madame Montanari was known as a London Doll Manufacturer from about 1849, and her stall at the Crystal Palace at the exhibition in Hyde Park in 1851 was described in the following words:

This stall consists of a series of dolls, representing all ages, from infancy to womanhood, arranged in several family groups, with suitable and elegant model furniture. These dolls have the hair, eyelashes and eye lids separately inserted in the wax, and are in other respects modelled with life-like truthfulness. Much skill is also evinced in the variety of expression which is given to these figures, in regard to the ages and stations which they are intended to represent.

'Younger' dolls were modelled as likenesses to the children of the Royal Family.

Some of these dolls were the ones which were sold at 5 guineas undressed, and were sold at a greatly increased price when richly attired. It has been said that the Montanari dolls were as well known for their clothes with the careful attention to detail, as they were for their actual make, and the beautifully attired dolls certainly fetched a still higher price than their undressed sisters. These garments were also noticed at the various exhibitions at which the dolls were shown and duly praised. The smaller undressed ones cost about 10s. each, but all the Montanari dolls were for the children of the wealthy, rather than for general sale.

Mention should also be made that the eyes of these wax dolls were of the glass paperweight variety, and were put into the hollow heads, and when the eyes focused correctly, they were fixed in position by a drop of wax. These eyes could be bought ready made.

Sometimes metal eyelets were used to protect the wax holes, but often these worked loose and had to be replaced. Strands of white thread, three maybe, or tape was used to fasten the waxen portions to the stuffed bodies, which went a little way into the hollow limbs for strength.

While Madame Montanari specialized in the making of dolls, Napoleon, who also gave his address as 29 Upper Charlotte Street, specialized in wax figures. He too, like Augusta, made some of the larger dolls, and his wax figures received attention at the Crystal Palace Exhibition of 1851. They were both careful in the way in which they inserted the hairs on the wax heads, and some of them were arranged to simulate a centre parting which was the fashion of the time, the dresses also being right up to date.

It was at this exhibition that Monsieur Napoleon Montanari showed a collection of figures illustrating the different characters of Mexican town and savage life, with their varied costumes and attributes. There were twelve figures of civilized Indians of Mexico and its environs, laden with produce and manufactures, and twelve savage Indians, male and female, called Mecos, inhabitants of the interior of Mexico. These were exhibited under glass domes on stands. Apart from other figures he also showed some rather gruesome incidents, one being a North American Indian preparing to scalp a white traveller, and another of an Indian carrying away a white child, as well as the anatomical figure mentioned earlier on.

Although Madame Augusta manufactured her dolls for about 36 years, which seems a long time, many of them must have been broken and not put together again, while others may have perished with heat, which was the fate of so many of these waxen dolls. It was probably this which made the Montanaris experiment with a thin, fine muslin over the wax, but in 1855 this idea 'which appeared to be good, had not the sanction of the customs'. Actually this idea was never brought to perfection and the dolls' faces look far from nice when the muslin begins to split, which indeed it did. However, they also made many wax dolls without the transparent muslin and many others of material only. These were of different textures, being made of fabric throughout, so they were as lasting as the good old 'rag-dolls' and very suitable for rough play in the nursery. Another thing in their favour was the price, as they sold for anything between 6s. 6d. and 30s.. including the dresses. Like the wax dolls they were made with skill, and commented on at the exhibitions where they were shown.

By 1855, Augusta was making larger dolls, to which she gave the same careful attention to detail as before.

Apart from dolls, Napoleon Montanari also made other things for children, such as toy animals, toy bells and musical toys, and in 1859, when he was living at Charles Street, Soho Square, he invented an apparatus which he claimed would enable young children to learn to walk. This was a kind of frame which came up to about the waist of the child (rather like the early ones one sees in engravings) but was made of rods on a stand which was fitted with casters, his idea being that it would prevent the child from falling when on its feet. Musical wires could be let into the spaces and in his words 'the seat may be provided with a utensil for the convenience of the child'.

He must have been an interesting character, possibly keen on history, clever with his fingers, and perhaps it was watching his own child, Richard Napoleon, learning to walk, that made him think of the apparatus. In any case, I should think Madame would be glad of something in the nature of a playpen while she was busy with her doll-making.

What intrigues me is the picture of Napoleon making his full-size anatomical specimens, while perhaps his wife is modelling one of her famous wax dolls, with their son Richard watching. Maybe he thought out the idea of covering his own wax dolls with muslin to make them stronger when he found that the dolls which his mother made were rather fragile.

In 1862, Augusta Montanari gives her address as 198 Oxford Street, London, and at the International Exhibition she again shows her model wax dolls and model rag dolls, this time stating that they were made 'with all modern improvements', and often equipped with both day and party frocks.

Later, back near Fitzroy Square again, but this time at 70 Warren Street, Richard Montanari, in 1869, is busy with the wholesale manufacture of dolls, both wax ones and rag ones, still of a high quality and winning prizes at various exhibitions, again bringing international fame to this family of doll-makers.

MONTANARI DOLLS AT THE GREAT EXHIBITION IN HYDE PARK, 1851
The Crystal Palace, published in penny parts by W. M. Clark.

'In the North Transept Gallery, Class 29, Case 122, were a rich display of model wax and rag dolls, by Madame Montanari. These playthings are indeed very beautifully modelled; the hair inserted into the head, eyelashes and eyebrows. They represent the different stages of childhood, up to womanhood, and were arranged in the case so as to form interesting family groups. They include portraits of several of the Royal children. The interior of the case represents a model drawing-room, the model furniture being carved and gilt, and elaborately finished.

The model rag dolls, in an adjoining small glass case, were a newly invented article, by Madame Montanari, peculiarly adapted for the nursery, for their softness and durability, and are largely patronized by those who are connoisseurs in dolls'-flesh.

The beautiful groups of Mexican figures exhibited by Montanari, in the Fine Art Court, daily attracted a throng of admiring gazers. They were indeed very interesting, as illustrating town and savage life in Mexico in all their phases. Amongst them the most remarkable were a grotesque figure of an 'Aguador' (water carrier), a Remendor or street cobbler in his ragged attire, a 'Confessional' group of three figures, a group of two Indian women dancing a fandango on the green, while the leper is playing on the guitar, and the scene in the courtyard of a farm, with the wealthy farmer and his lady about to set out on a journey. A beautiful group of Mexican fruits (50 in number, natural size) formed an interesting feature.

We have already spoken of M. Montanari's collection of Mexican figures and of Madame Montanari's wonderful dolls, of which latter we presented our readers with a group. We now give a miniature representation of some 2 to 3 dozen of the Mexican figures, productions copied with extreme accuracy of form and colour after local originals, and therefore extremely interesting, as well as ornamental. We cannot help remarking, when contemplating these very accurate and amusing productions, and recollecting the equally remarkable models in the Indian department, that the power of imitation to an extent almost to be delusive is compatible with the total absence of all those higher principles which constitute the vitality of high art.'

(I am afraid there is no signature under these remarks, but the last is very interesting, considering when it was written.)

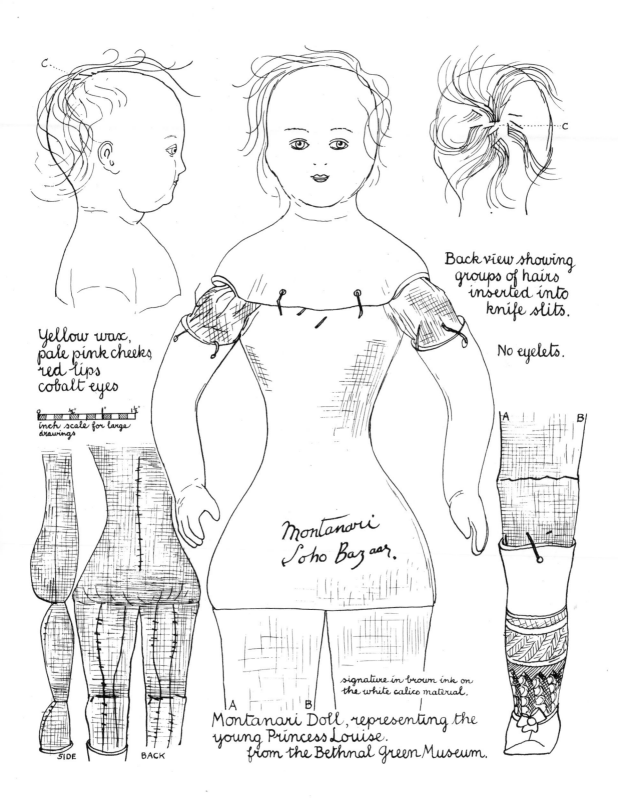

C

Yellow wax,
pale pink cheeks,
red lips
cobalt eyes

inch scale for large
drawings

SIDE   BACK

Back view showing
groups of hairs
inserted into
knife slits.

No eyelets.

C

Montanari
Soho Bazaar.

signature in brown ink on
the white calico material.

A   B

Montanari Doll, representing the
young Princess Louise,
from the Bethnal Green Museum.

A   B

ARMAND MARSEILLE

The dolls of Armand Marseille were well known at the end of the 19th and the beginning of the 20th centuries. Made in Germany, they have his initials, together with a number, usually on the back of the neck or just underneath the hair which can often be pushed back to reveal the number.

He made 'black' dolls as well as 'white' ones in various sizes, and many of his early dolls are finding their way into museums, though others are too recent and are probably still tucked away in the drawers, trunks and attics of private houses, or may still be played with today.

An Armand Marseille doll of 1890 would have a bisque head and jointed leather body. Some would have kid hands and feet, and later ones, still retaining the kid body, would have arms and hands of bisque with ball joints at the elbow and a joint at the shoulder and at the wrist.

There are a few dolls by him in Pollock's Toy Museum at Monmouth Street, Cambridge Circus, and more in the London Museum, Kensington Palace.

One of his dolls at the turn of the century had a jointed kid body with a gadget for saying 'Aah'. The length of this doll was about 26 inches, but the head was very small, being only about $3\frac{1}{2}$ inches high, which was small in scale for a doll of this period. The one I have drawn was bought in Paris.

Later dolls of round about 1908 or 1909 had hair carefully stitched on to canvas in circles, and this hair could be washed and then waved with curling tongs heated across methylated-spirit lamps. The eyes were inset, and opened and shut, the lids being part of the eyeball, which was the usual manner at this time. The bodies of these dolls were of pink canvas and stuffed, the lower arms of bisque with fingers, and the lower leg just made to imitate a black stocking and stuffed. This did away with the job of making feet, and socks and shoes for these dolls could be bought in any toy shop and in all sizes.

A doll of about 1911 would have a bisque head, but wooden body, arms and legs, and the composition hands well made, and the legs of covered wood below the knee. Again the eyes would open and shut by means of an inside weight.

Every doll coming to England had to be stamped with the mark 'MADE IN GERMANY' (or any other country of their origin) after the year 1890, and most of the Marseille ones are stamped in this way, and with a number.

I like the Armand Marseille dolls; I think they have nice expressions. My own, when I was small, had fair hair and large brown eyes.

370.
A.M.3.DEP.
made in Germany.

Sign on back of neck

Strands of hair on canvas

inch scale. Dolls' heads by Armand Marseille   about 1910

HERR STEINER

Rudolf Steiner was another clever doll-maker, interested mostly in the mechanical possibilities of these playthings and inventing a good many ideas of his own.

In 1863, in France, a mechanical Steiner doll was made, and in 1869 automatic toys and velocipedes were made by a toy manufacturer, one Jules Nicolas Steiner, who lived in the Rue de Saintonge, Paris.

In 1889, Rudolf Steiner of Thuringia in Germany made what I should think would be the very first doll who could drink from a bottle. This doll was provided with a syphon which passed through the head so that the liquid contained in the bottle could be withdrawn from the latter into a receptacle when the syphon was set in action by sucking a small quantity of the liquid through the nozzle. The conduit consisted of a syphon, the longer leg of which was situated at the back of the doll. The doll sat in a chair, and the liquid passed through the doll's head, down behind her hair, into a box in the seat of her chair or into a receptacle. I should think, looking at the drawing, that she almost had the modern American dolls beaten at the job, and this was over sixty years ago. All the same, I think this one is a pretty repulsive-looking creature.

Steiner also made some rather bald-looking baby dolls which could walk. They had open mouths showing tiny teeth, and on the base of the shoulder would be his signature mark, Rudolf Steiner.

Doll's eyes, 1880, patented in Germany, No.14292 by Jules Nicolas Steiner of Paris.

Walking doll 1902, patented in the U.S.A. No. 695121, by Edmund Ulrich Steiner

Feeding doll, 1889, by Rudolf Steiner English patent, No.14534

CHARLES MARSH

Charles Marsh was a maker of dolls in London from about 1870 onwards. His dolls were very English-looking, with fair, flowing hair and forget-me-not blue eyes. He set his hair into the wax heads in rather thick groups of hairs and suggested a vague parting in the centre. Somehow this makes the dolls more childlike in appearance and not quite so ladylike. The little mouths are painted a deep pink and at the nostrils are two red dots. The eyes are inset, not the paperweight variety, but a good clear cobalt blue, with inset eyelashes and eyebrows of real hair.

The flesh-colour wax used for the heads is pinker than that used for the arms and legs, and there is no indication of pinker cheeks, though there may have been at the time of making. As dolls go, the ears are bigger than usual, but are mostly hidden under the thick corn-coloured hair.

They are chubby dolls with the suggestion of a double chin and a fold where the neck meets the shoulders. The limbs are of hollow wax, a yellowish colour with two holes at the arm above the elbow, and two at the leg just above the knee. There is one crease at the elbow joint and the fingers are close together, the thumb being outstretched. The nails appear to have been pressed into a groove with a small shaped tool, and the toe-nails are the same.

The hollow head, neck and shoulders are in one piece and joined to the body by thread being passed through the two holes found on the back and the front. The body is a stuffed one made of strong white linen. There are no eyelets in the holes through the wax, and the bodies are stitched flat across, where the legs join, in the usual way, to enable the doll to take a sitting position.

The blue stamp on the body is very interesting and indicates that Charles Marsh supplied dolls to E. Moody, and it was from the latter that the wax doll in the London Museum was purchased. He made dolls until about 1895, and Mrs Mary Ann Marsh carried on till about 1900.

There was an S. Marsh who made dolls in 1898, and even decided to take out a patent, but somehow this idea never materialized, and whether he was a relation of the Charles or the Mary Ann Marsh I do not know, though he certainly made dolls at this time. It would have been a most interesting specification to read if only he had carried it out.

Charles Marsh. His sign pale blue on white, sometimes also the words 'Corinthian Bazaar, Argyll Street, London W'

DEAN'S RAG BOOK CO. LTD

In England, the rag dolls made by this company at High Path, Merton, London, are well known, and at the beginning of the 19th century most little girls would have a rag doll of some kind amongst the other dolls in the nursery. In the U.S.A., up to 1885, all the rag dolls had been made at home, but in 1900 a patent was taken out for a Doll made of Rag, so it must have been much the same in both countries.

One of the first rag dolls printed in a sheet in 1903 was about 24 inches high when made up and stuffed, and it would stand a good deal of hard wear and knocking about, in fact a good everyday doll to play with, while looking forward to Sunday, when perhaps the 'best doll' would be brought out again for an airing.

Mr R. E. Ellett, director of the Dean's Rag Book Co., writes:

Our first dolls were a natural corollary to the Rag Books, the first of which appeared in 1903: they were printed on sheets of cotton cloth just like the books themselves, and were sold in that form with instructions how to cut them out, sew them together and stuff them.

Subsequently, it was found that relatively few people would take the trouble to do this, and we set about making the dolls up and stuffing them ourselves. Various improvements were rapidly introduced until the so-called 'Rag Dolls' became really beautiful creations, challenging dolls made by various other methods.

. . . Fifty dolls were shown at the *Daily Express* Exhibition, 1922, and . . . The British Industries Fair in 1946 . . . and we enclose a copy of the earliest Rag Doll Sheet of which we retain any record.

It should be emphasized that both the 1922 and 1946 dolls here shown (photographs were enclosed) are 'Rag' dolls in the true sense of the word, being made of textile materials: the beautiful faces are made of cotton cloth, the contours being obtained by embossing between bronze dies.

The only exceptions to this are the hands, which are moulded in unbreakable material because the detail of these parts is too fine to be obtained by embossing.

Unfortunately Mr Ellett, who wished me success with my book, saying: 'This fascinating subject has been sadly neglected by historians in the past,' has since died, and Deans have now closed down their department for making rag dolls (1958), so these rag dolls have now joined the other playthings of bygone days.

WHAT THE WORLD'S WOMEN ARE WEARING. *Daily Express* Women's Exhibition, 1922

A very remarkable series of dolls dressed to display a microcosm of present-day costume in other parts of the world is attracting much attention at the *Daily Express* Women's Exhibition, now open at Olympia.

What other women wear is already intriguing enough when it is merely a question of the woman next door, the latest fashionable bride, or the leaders of the Paris mode, but these fade into insignificance beside the fathomless mysteries of the Orient and the weird and wildly colourful combinations of beads and blanket that clothe or do not clothe the ebon beauties of Central Africa.

These and many others may be studied at close range in this section. It will, moreover, enable mere man, if he will give himself the trouble, to discover at last what is meant by a 'Magyar' blouse and a 'Geisha' sleeve, what a basque is and why so called: whence come those marvellous colour discords known as 'Batik' and numerous equally absorbing matters.

Visitors who pay the tribute of a close and attentive scrutiny to the remarkable attire of these dolls will not fail to notice the wonderful and ingenious way in which they have been contrived so that each not only has a distinct personality in perfect harmony with its outer trappings, but can be and is posed with perfect naturalness so as to carry off its accoutrements with the utmost effect.

It is comforting to know that where the clothes have been collected with much care and trouble from all corners of the globe, the little wearers themselves – the dolls that have been specially chosen to display these exotic trappings – have been made in England, and a study of them should do something to refute the idea current in some quarters that the best dolls inevitably come from Germany.

Not the least interesting incident in the organization of the Women's Exhibition was the search among the great doll-makers of the world for a suitable miniature mannequin to display this interesting series of costumes, a search which ended in triumph at the Elephant and Castle headquarters of those wizards of the doll world, Dean's Rag Book Company Ltd.

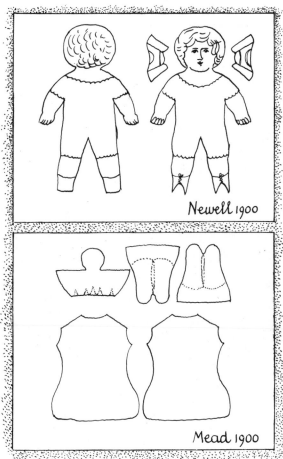

Newell 1900

Mead 1900

Contempory patterns for rag dolls from the U.S.A. printed on sheets.

THE STREET-SELLERS OF DOLLS

Extract from *Mayhew's London*, 1851: The making of dolls, like that of many a thing required for a mere recreation, a toy, a pastime, is often carried on amidst squalor, wretchedness or privation, or to use the word I have frequently heard among the poor, 'pinching'.

Dolls are now so cheap, and so generally sold by open-air traders whose wares are of a miscellaneous character, as among the 'Swagbarrow' or 'penny-a-piece' men, that the sale of what are among the most ancient of all toys, as a business in itself, is far smaller, numerically, than it was.

The dolls are most usually carried in baskets by street-sellers (who are not makers) and generally by women who are very poor. Here and there in the streets most frequented by the patrons of the open-air trade may be seen a handsome stall of dolls of all sizes and fashions, but these are generally the property of the makers, although those makers may buy a small portion of their stock. There are also small stalls which may present the stock of the mere seller.

The dolls for street traffic may be bought at the swag-shops or of the makers. For the little armless penny dolls, the maker charges the street-seller eight pennies, and to the swag-shop keeper who may buy largely, $7\frac{1}{2}d$. the dozen. Some little stalls are composed entirely of penny dolls, on others the price runs from a penny to sixpence. The chief trade, however, among the class I now describe is carried on by the display of dolls in baskets. If the vendor can only attract the notice of children, and more especially in a private suburban residence where children are not used to the sight of dolls on stalls or barrows, or in shops, and can shower a few blessings and compliments: 'God be wid your bhutiful faces thin, and yours too, my lady, ma'am' (with a curtsey to mistress or maid). 'Buy one of these dolls off a poor woman, shure they're bhutiful dolls and shuted for them angels o' the worruld.' Under such circumstances, I say, a sale is almost certain.

A vendor of dolls expresses an opinion that as long as ever there are children from two years old to ten, there will always be purchasers of dolls. 'But for all that,' said he, 'somehow or other 'tis nothing of a trade to what it used to be. Spoiled children are our best customers. Whenever we see a likely customer approaching, we that is who know the business, always throw ourselves in the way, and spread out our dolls to the best advantage. If we hear young miss say SHE WILL have one, and cries for it, we are almost sure of a customer, and if we see her kick and fight a bit with the nuss-maid we are sure of a good price. Most of the doll-sellers are the manufacturers of the dolls, that is, I mean they puts 'em together. The heads are made in Hawlburgh. The principal places for buying them in London are at Alfred Davis's in Houndsditch, White's in Houndsditch and Joseph's in Leadenhall Street.'

STREET-SELLERS OF GUTTA-PERCHA HEADS

. . . the elastic toys called 'gutta-percha heads'; these, however, have no gutta-percha in their composition, but consist solely of a composition made of glue and treacle, the same as is used for printers' rollers. The heads are small coloured models of the human face, usually with projecting nose and chin, and a wide or distorted mouth, which admit of being squeezed into different forms of features, their elasticity causing them to return to the original caste. The trade carried on in the streets in these toys was at one time extensive, but it seems now to be gradually disappearing.'

THE DOLL'S-EYE MAKER

A curious part of the street toy business is the sale of dolls, and especially that odd branch of it, doll's-eye making. There are only two persons following this business in London, and by the most intelligent of these I was furnished with the following curious information. – 'I make all kinds of eyes,' the eye-manufacturer said, 'both doll's and human eyes, birds' eyes are mostly manufactured in Birmingham. Of dolls' eyes there are two sorts, the common and the natural as we call it. The common are simply small hollow glass spheres, made of white enamel, and coloured either black or blue, for only two colours of these are made. The better-most dolls' eyes, or the natural ones, are made in a superior manner, but after a similar fashion to the commoner sort.'   Mayhew, 1851

I have read of a mother who wore a doll's glass eye in the bun at the back of her hair. In this way she kept an eye on her children, who literally believed that she had 'eyes in the back of her head'.

Jumeau doll, cream kid body, bisque head, swivel neck, blue eyes with white lines, fawn painted eyelashes and eyebrows, nut brown wig, pink nostrils, mouth and cheeks, kid fitting very carefully over shoulders. 17 in. high
London Museum

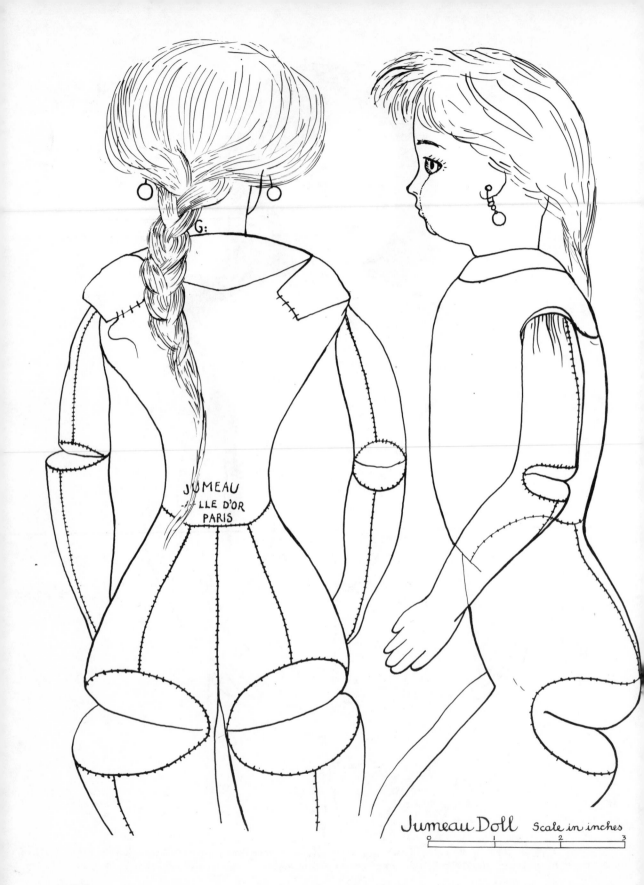

JUMEAU
LLE D'OR
PARIS

Jumeau Doll Scale in inches

Details of Jumeau doll
in the London Museum.
Doll's head and boots of
same period. Hollow bisque
head filled with cork, hair
sewn to canvas, swivel neck,
inset eyes of dark blue with
faint lines, very flat pierced
ears, pink cheeks, white kid
body, separate fingers. The
kid fits carefully over the
shoulders.   Scale in inches

0   1   2   3   4

Pierotti wax doll, with inset hair. 22 in. long
Named Patrick Enrico, and dressed by Miss Muriel Pierotti when a child

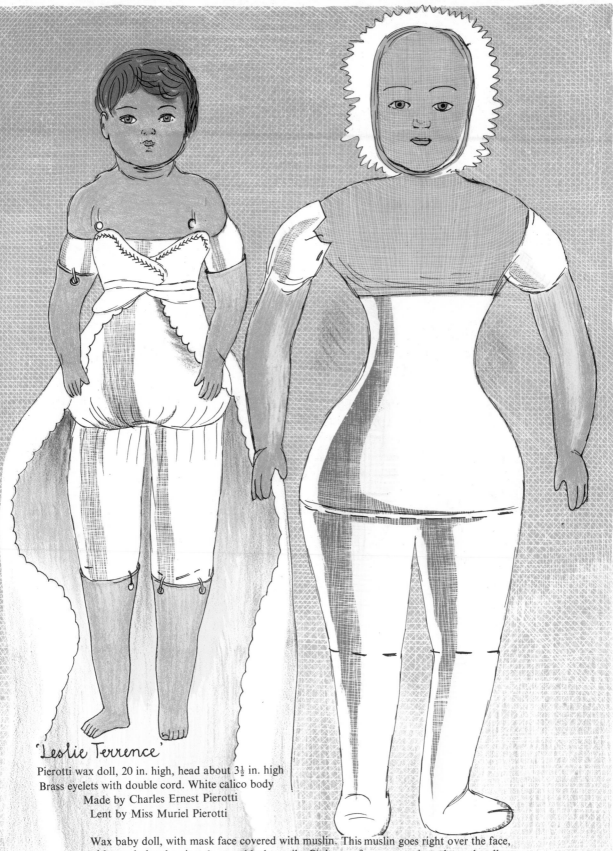

'Leslie Terrence'
Pierotti wax doll, 20 in. high, head about 3½ in. high
Brass eyelets with double cord. White calico body
Made by Charles Ernest Pierotti
Lent by Miss Muriel Pierotti

Wax baby doll, with mask face covered with muslin. This muslin goes right over the face,
with two holes showing the two black pupils. Pink wax forearms to just above the elbow
Said to have been purchased at the 1851 Exhibition. (Might be a Montanari.) London Museum

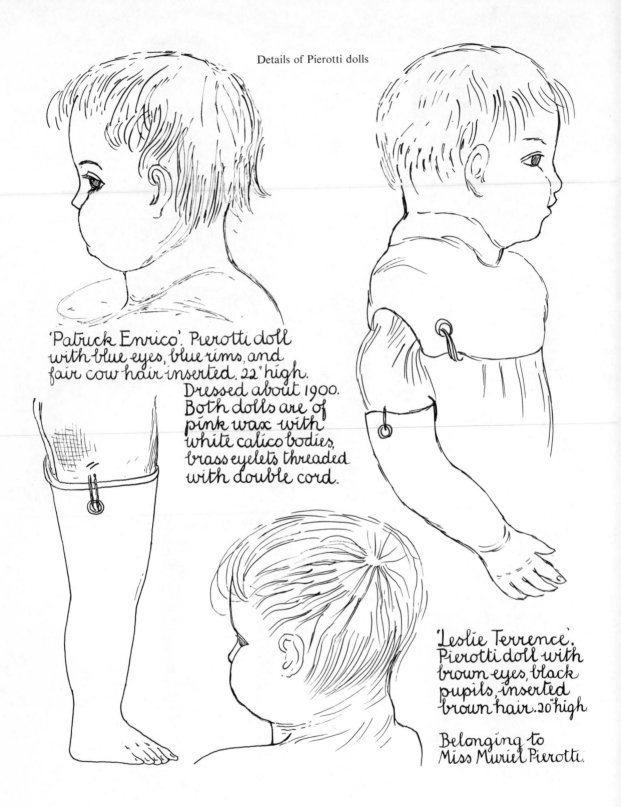

'Patrick Enrico'. Pierotti doll
with blue eyes, blue rims, and
fair cow hair inserted. 22" high.
Dressed about 1900.
Both dolls are of
pink wax with
white calico bodies,
brass eyelets threaded
with double cord.

'Leslie Terrence'.
Pierotti doll with
brown eyes, black
pupils, inserted
brown hair. 20" high

Belonging to
Miss Muriel Pierotti.

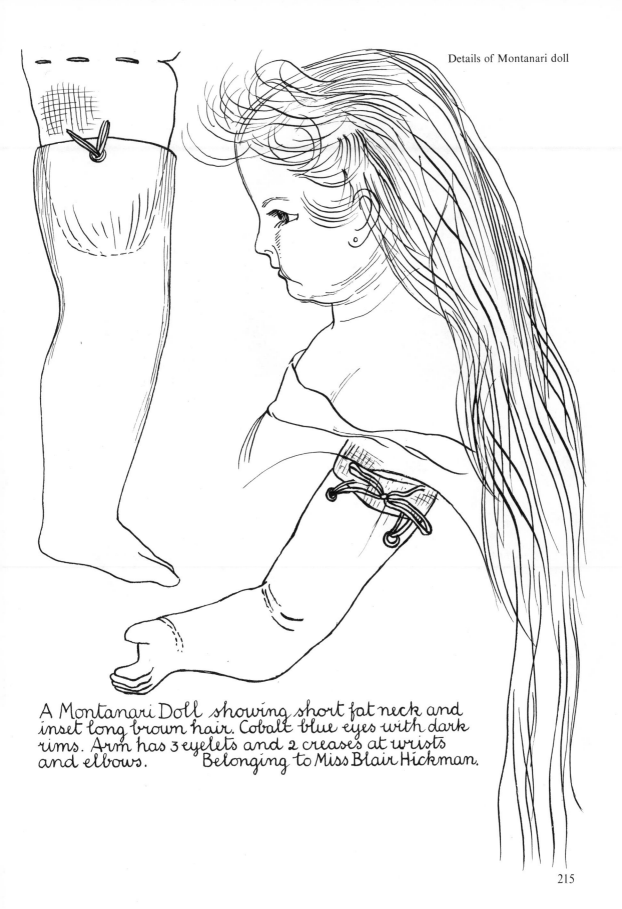

A Montanari Doll showing short fat neck and inset long brown hair. Cobalt blue eyes with dark rims. Arm has 3 eyelets and 2 creases at wrists and elbows.　　　　Belonging to Miss Blair Hickman.

Montanari wax doll, 1858. The white embroidered dress comes to the knee. 22 in. high, named 'Edith'.
Given by Mrs. Pember to the London Museum

Montanari do

Montanari wax doll, with long light brown hair. 26 in. high.
Lent by Miss Irene Blair Hickman

Crystal Palace

Montanari
wax doll
1864

Doll by Heinrich Handwerck.

BÉBÉ
COSMOPOLITE

10 x

A Bru sleeping doll 1890

Jumeau baby doll showing eye
with painted eyebrow and a
pronounced top to the ear. Arm
has no wrist joint. The higher
the number, the smaller the size.

Lent by Miss Irene Blair Hickman

Details of doll by Charles Marsh

showing toe nails pressed in groove, 2 holes in waist arms, and 2 in legs, but no eyelets

0" |————————| 1" inch scale

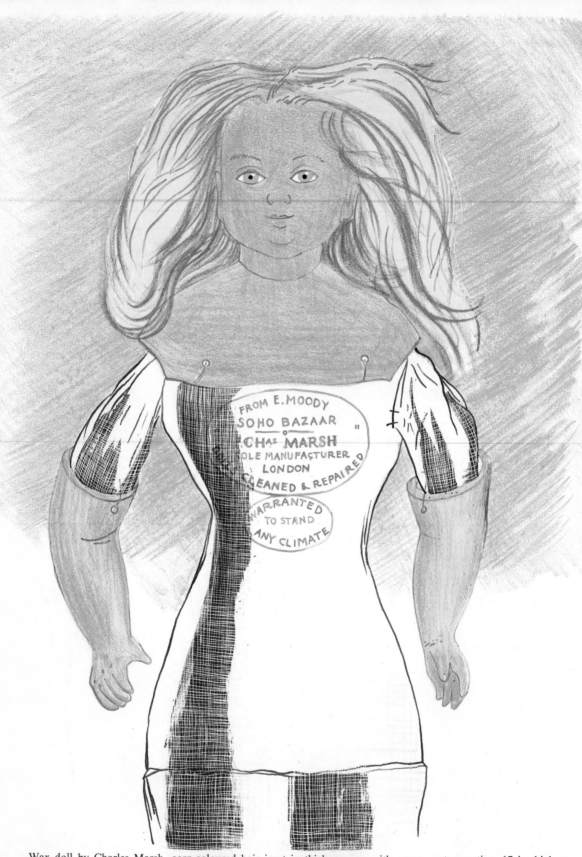

FROM E. MOODY
SOHO BAZAAR
CHAS MARSH
OLE MANUFACTURER
LONDON
CLEANED & REPAIRED

WARRANTED
TO STAND
ANY CLIMATE

Wax doll by Charles Marsh, corn-coloured hair inset in thick groups, with vague centre parting, 17 in. high
London Museum

Designs for Dolly's Dresses.

London A. N. Myers & Co. 13 Berners St. Oxford St. W.

Designs for Dollys Dresses from a little portfolio. *Dollys Dressmaker* Part II, Third edition
Published by A. N. Myers & Co, 15 Berners Street, London, and by Winckelmann & Sons, Berlin

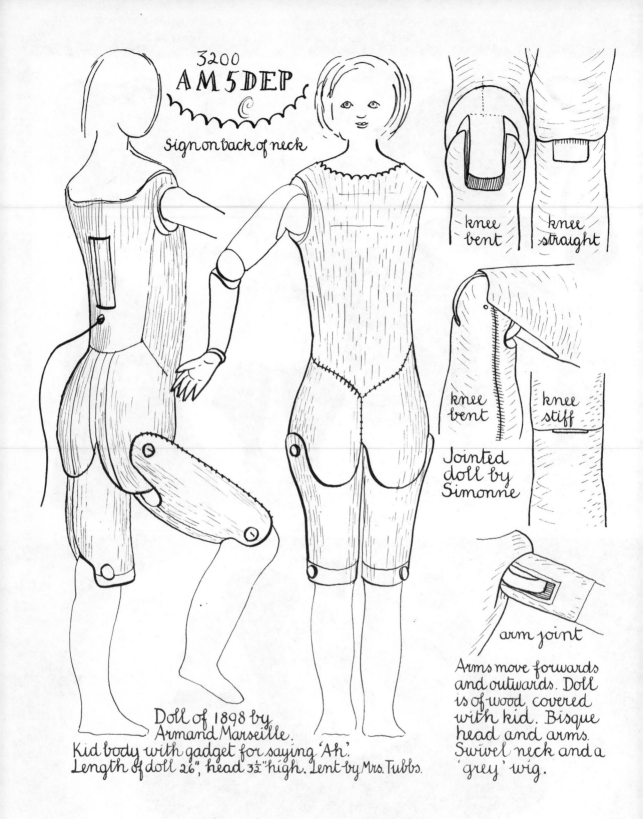

3200
AM 5 DEP

sign on back of neck

knee bent   knee straight

knee bent   knee stiff

Jointed doll by Simonne

arm joint

Arms move forwards and outwards. Doll is of wood, covered with kid. Bisque head and arms. Swivel neck and a 'grey' wig.

Doll of 1898 by Armand Marseille.
Kid body with gadget for saying 'Ah'.
Length of doll 26", head 3½" high. Lent by Mrs. Tubbs.

White silk taffeta edged with lace

White muslin edged with lace

White linen with one tuck and crochet edging

Cream flannel with scarlet wool blanket stitch

White linen drawers
edged with crochet

black shoes, brown soles.
Details of Doll on pages 174 and 175

Armand Marseille
wooden doll of 1915
Made in Germany.

Lent by Mrs Gordon Coles

'Dorothy Monica'

Arm of
doll on
page 173.

A big baby doll by Dean's Rag Book Co. 1903. This is one of the dolls which were printed on material and sold in order that they could be made up at home and then stuffed. This is an English rag doll of entirely British manufacture, printed on linen, 30 in. across, 28½ in. down, together with three smaller dolls, Old King Cole, Lucy Locket, Little Dutch doll, with all directions for making up and stuffing, printed in three languages. The 'Big Baby Doll' is complete with Tru Shu feet

A felt doll of about 1935. Height 12½ in. Hair inset in groups. Dressed as a pink rose in shaded muslin with picot edging. All clothes take on and off. Her mother's doll, lent by Miss Anne Weston

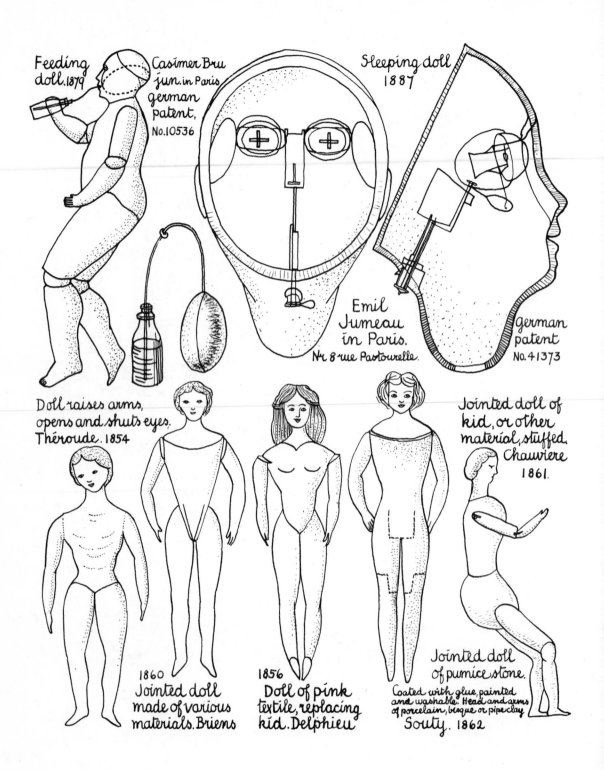

Feeding doll. 1879

Casimer Bru jun. in Paris. german patent. No. 10536

Sleeping doll 1887

Emil Jumeau in Paris. Nr 8 rue Pastourelle.

german patent No. 41373

Doll raises arms, opens and shuts eyes. Théroude. 1854

Jointed doll of kid, or other material, stuffed. Chauviere 1861.

1860 Jointed doll made of various materials. Briens

1856 Doll of pink textile, replacing kid. Delphieu

Jointed doll of pumice stone. Coated with glue, painted and washable. Head and arms of porcelain, bisque or pipe clay Souty. 1862

DOLLS OF MANY KINDS

In England, Pedlar dolls were made by Messrs Evans and Cartwright of Wolverhampton. They made papier-mâché dolls in vast numbers and in twelve sizes. By 1830 the bodies were improved by press moulding, stove drying and varnishing, and the dolls were cheaper to buy. Even at this period they were sought after as ornaments, and the tiny miniature objects on their trays treated with great care. Some of these dolls were placed under glass domes, and the museums of Bethnal Green, Colchester, and Luton have some good examples.

In the 1840's, many doll patents were concerned with moulding dolls and with the use of rubber.

Thomas Forster improved the use of India rubber by casting it in moulds for parts of dolls in 1844, and Edward Payne, in 1849, moulded and joined hollow figures, such as children's dolls. A piece of the compound was boiled until it was in a soft state ready for a mould. Each figure consisted of a front mould, a back mould and a back core. The moulds were made to act upon the material by means of pressure. In joining the shells thus formed, a red-hot heater for an Italian iron was applied to the edge or rims of the shells, which were then pressed together and trimmed. This compound was made of gutta-percha, chopped fine, masticated in water containing salt and oil of vitriol, and boiled, and then pressed, brushed, hammered and rolled.

Jean Quiquandon devised a machine about 1850 for making cork powder, which was used for the stuffing of dolls, and Edouard Guichard ornamented dolls and children's playthings by using flock and thereby giving a soft surface to the various articles, but this gradually wore off with use.

Although the wax and the composition dolls were made in the United Kingdom, the wooden dolls were imported in 1851, and the papier-mâché heads all came from abroad. The bodies of the dolls were made in this country, and the whole doll assembled here.

In 1858, Richard Brooman improved the manufacture of dolls by using vulcanized caoutchouc. He made a metal mould, hermetically sealed it, and a ball of caoutchouc was put within and locked in the mould. It was plunged in hot vulcanizing composition, enough for a doll, and expanded with the heat. This doll was made in two parts, a top half and a bottom half, the joins being covered with a belt.

Charles Rostaing made dolls' heads from a mixture of gutta-percha and other substances, which could be 'diversely coloured', and which were so hard that he claimed that the substance replaced wood.

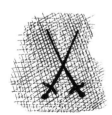

Shows mark on Meissen China head
1800

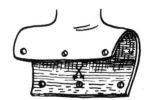

Meissen China, sign in underglaze blue,
marked on a doll's shoulder

Henri d'Allemagne gives a description of dolls in the year 1844; 'Most of the dolls made at this time are of moulded cardboard and only the hands are of cut-out wood. The limbs are attached by rubber bands.' He describes the eyes as being of shining blue pottery, and the hair painted on the cardboard in symmetrical, regular curls. There were also leather-covered babies, stuffed with wood sawdust, but their wax heads came from England.

Other doll-makers were mentioned in the 'Citations Favorables' on the French Exhibition of 1844. M. Kopp of Paris in the rue du Temple was mentioned for a collection of playthings and 'above all for his gay model of a dining-room with sideboard and furnished table.' Madame Anna Cécile François of the rue du Faubourg-du-Temple, Paris, was mentioned for the fabrication of 'little dolls serving as actors in the children's theatres'. The dolls of M. Brouillet were said to be agreeable to little girls who wished to cut and sew clothes, and M. Colin of Paris received an honourable mention for his small toys and articles for dolls' houses. The Belton and the Jumeau dolls were also mentioned at this exhibition.

In 1843 M. Petit took out a patent for a china doll, but wax heads were still purchased from England. 'Cardboard' bodies were produced in thousands, selling at the wholesale price of about 23 centimes a dozen.

Arnaud, a well-known doll-maker, brought out a jointed doll in 1852 and another in 1864.

The millboard paste poured into the moulds for dolls in 1550 had been known as 'D'oyselet'. Now, in 1849, Madame Montanari poured wax into moulds in order to make dolls from solid wax. Later, she poured the wax over a metal foundation, or one of papier-mâché, and later still she made dolls with a composition base and poured the wax over this.

Mademoiselle Calixte Huret, a Parisian doll-maker, made hers with gutta-percha bodies, to which she fixed an imported head from Germany. France often imported heads, wax ones from England, and papier-mâché from Germany. Using porcelain heads on her jointed dolls, Mademoiselle Huret at first intended selling the dolls only, but soon she set up a whole industry employing a number of people to make the various items of clothes needed for a doll's complete wardrobe. The gutta-percha bodies had strong joints, and the porcelain heads were finished with a spherical part to permit movement.

By 1851 the market for dolls became so crowded that the prices were very, very low. Dressed dolls, including a bonnet, were bought for as little as 8d. a dozen, and undressed dolls of composition were sold for 2½d. a dozen. There were ninety master doll-makers, employing 805 people, and the value of the trade was placed at about £48,358.

M. Greffier made talking dolls in 1855, and other dolls which were known as the 'Japonese' type and were referred to as babies. Patents for joints were taken out by M. Roy, mechanical dolls by Hammond, india-rubber dolls by d'Autremont, and in the same year an interesting patent was taken out for enamel eyes.

Charles Bertram, 4 rue des Archives, Paris. Toys, 1878.
Manufacturer of the swimming doll or 'poupée nageuse'
called 'Ondine'

Rubber joints by Arnaud
French patent
NO. 13255

Many mechanical dolls, puppets and automata came during the 1860's. William Clark invented a walking doll and so did Alfred Newton and Joseph Munn. In 1866 David Lee made ball-and-socket joints for dolls which were connected with springs, and could be used for lay figures, dolls and manikins. Clivell patented a moving doll and John Pepper made gymnastic figures. Barcelonnettes and cradles for dolls were made by Jean Mougin.

Not all the specifications registered at the Patent Office were actually patented, but where there are diagrams they are interesting. The wording takes you back into the past, and the patents are a definite way of determining the date of a doll, as nothing could be patented if it had been done before.

At the International Exhibition held in 1862, Thomas Peacock, of 515 New Oxford Street, showed dolls which he styled as 'Model and Composition Dolls'. He said that he manufactured all kinds of these dolls, and that he had on hand a stock of a thousand, dressed and undressed, from which to select. He supplied single dolls at wholesale prices, ranging from £1 to £5.

George Burley of 28 George Street, Blackfriars Road, Southwark, made dolls 'of a novel description', what I do not know, but the dolls which won a bronze medal at this exhibition were those made by Henry and Celia Pierotti. They worked at 13 Mortimer Street, off Oxford Street, and Celia showed Foreign and English toys, while Henry showed wax model dolls with inserted hair, together with other dolls and wax figures.

Morrell's had a toyshop in Oxford Street, near Stratford Place, which made special displays of dolls about Christmas time. The windows were dressed with a Christmas tree, on the top of which would be a fairy doll, complete with crown and wand, and a star on her head. Other dolls were arranged around the tree, some in beds, others in perambulators and some just lying back in their boxes. Baby dolls were dressed in long clothes, with bonnets trimmed with swansdown, and other dolls were dressed in party frocks.

About 1823, dolls could be made to say 'Papa' and 'Maman' by squeezing their hands, and Monsieur d'Allemagne mentions dolls which talked according to which arm was raised. Dolls made by M. Bru had an internal organ permitting the body to move forward, backward and sideways, and these were made of kid with a groove in the upper leg. Maelzel invented a speaking doll which he patented in France in 1824.

An advertisement states that 'Pour six francs je remue les yeux et je tourne la tête' while for the sum of 10 francs, 'Je dis Papa et Maman'.

In the Paris Exhibition of 1844, there were dolls made by M. Belton and M. Jumeau of the rue Salle-au-Comte. Other dolls were well made by M. Brouillet of 116 rue St Denis, who made dolls which could stand up on their own, and in addition he also made dolls' clothes.

John Wheeler, 15 Newgate Street, London
Toys, dolls and dolls' dresses. 1879

Emily Dorcas Godfrey, Sarah Godfrey and Catherine
Maria Godfrey, 30 George Street, Croydon, Surrey
Doll manufacturers. 1880

At the Paris Exhibition there were dolls that danced the polka, made by Théroude, and a doll, dressed in blue, which said 'Papa' and 'Maman', made by Giroux. Mlle Jenny Bereux, of Paris, showed dolls' trousseaux, and there were also Prussian dolls. Two stalls were devoted to dolls, and these were described by an Englishman visiting the Exhibition as 'having a tendency to reveal the various stages of the feminine toilet'.

This same Englishman seemed astonished at the dolls he saw at this Exhibition in Paris. He says, 'Here are cases of wonderful French dolls, which now appear to be simpering from every corner, inviting his attention – here, for instance are dolls of all kinds, dressed, or in that state in which beauty is said to be adorned the most. It would also appear that dolls marry, since here are elaborate trousseaux especially made for them, when accepted, possibly by some Jack-in-the-box, who appears to be leering from the next stall, in which the toys of P. Ringel of Paris, Rue de l'Oseille, are arranged – including (little visitors will be shocked to hear it) dolls bathing. Surely these dolls must have found their way here from Ramsgate!'

Clement made a doll of leather in 1863, and Lamour an automatic doll, and M. Bru made three, a crying doll in 1867, a puzzle doll in 1869, and in 1870 a magical doll. M. Chavire made a speaking doll, and a flying doll was made by M. Boutard.

Metal frames and joints were used by Pannier in 1872, and metal was again used by Vervelle in 1876. Others were made by Gerardin, in caoutchouc, a dancing doll by Schmetzer and one which could pull faces was made by Gerabon.

Heavy duty was paid on all the imported dolls from Germany and from England.

Ludwig Greiner made dolls of papier-mâché, with arms of leather and bodies stuffed with rags. In 1840 he was listed as a 'Toy man' in the Philadelphia Directory. A German immigrant, he may have been descended from the Greiner family of Thuringia, a town noted for its toys. This family founded a porcelain industry in 1764, and there were five sons, all potters.

Many rubber dolls come from America and, in 1856, the Goodyear rubber dolls were made in all sizes.

Rawhide dolls, made by Frank J. Darrow at Connecticut about 1860 and 1866, were of untanned leather, and were made by stretching leather over moulds, leaving it to dry, and then it was painted. The dolls looked nice when new, but if not well cared for they were nibbled at by mice, so they were not really a great success.

Philip Lerch made dolls about 1866 and 1875, and in this year the *Delineator Magazine* included patterns for making dolls' clothes, and girls could now 'prepare wardrobes for their dollies'.

Paper dolls were made of well-known actresses in 1880 and I should imagine these were larger than the

A. and J. Isaacs, 33 Houndsditch, London
Wholesale doll importers and dressers
Dolls dressed and undressed. 1887

Pewter toys. Henry Thomas Bull,
Newington Causeway, Surrey. 1888

tiny paper figures of Dickens characters in his house in Doughty Street, London, which can be seen today.

Many different kinds of joints were invented in the U.S.A., the most well known being those of J. A. H. Ellis of Springfield in 1873, and those of G. W. Sanders for tenon and mortise joints in 1880. The Pinto Collection of Wooden Bygones, at Northwood, near London, has a doll made in America by C. Schoenhut, about 1911.

Parsons made celluloid dolls with joints held together by wire springs; these dolls, made from scraps left over from celluloid collars, could float in water.

In 1880 a special method was developed for colouring the eyes of celluloid dolls; others were made wearing printed corsets. Flexible rubber dolls had soft wire frames, other dolls walked and talked. Hotchkiss, in 1875, made a clockwork walking doll. There was a talking and crying doll, which worked by blowing through a tube, and Bartenstein patented a double-faced doll in 1881, which wore a bonnet to hide the face not in use.

Pumice-stone was used in the finishing of dolls' heads, and Carpenter claimed a 'most beautiful and natural look' in his celluloid dolls where the eyebrows were incised and coloured before being rubbed down with pumice-stone. Monroe, another doll-maker, was the first to make a hard-rubber doll, with the ball-shaped head resting in a socket, secured by elastic bands.

Directions for making a 'Common Linen Doll' were given in a girl's book in 1881. Martha Wellington made rag dolls in 1883, and M. L. Mead patented a rag doll in 1900. Between 1905 and 1910, there were rag dolls printed on sheets in oils; these were for cutting out, machining and stuffing. Sometimes they were printed on cottons and sometimes on heavy sateens, the dolls mostly having golden hair, red stockings and black shoes. Patent gussets in the feet enabled these dolls to stand up on their own, some dolls being quite large, even 2½ feet high, in 1907. At the same time, rag dolls much like these could be purchased in England, sometimes ready stuffed and others to be stuffed at home.

The many dolls and dolls' heads which were imported from Germany could no longer come to America during the 1914–18 War, and small brass heads, which used to come, were now substituted by the use of tin. Moulds, belonging to the famous German company of Armand Marseille, were used by the Fulper Pottery Company, but their results were coarser than those of the Germans, and no more were made after 1920.

Gowdry's tumbler doll, in 1916, is interesting because it has legs, which is unusual in a doll of this type.

The Coleman walking dolls and the Fisher sitting dolls were made about this time and the well-known Bye-lo baby dolls came in 1920; also dolls with wooden heads and movable wooden eyes.

U.S.A. Patent

John Lord Hinde, Hinde Bros, 1a City Road, Finsbury, London
Brush manufacturer. Makes dolls. 1888
He made compressed pulp dolls between dies.

U.S.A. Patent

In Germany, 1860, the firm of Kestner was in existence, and by 1894 they were well known for their dolls. At first these dolls had kid bodies; later these were of strong muslin, and they also made jointed dolls, usually marked with the letters J D K.

Composition dolls were made by F. M. Schilling of Sonneberg, in Thuringia. Papier-mâché was used for the heads, arms and legs and the bodies were of cotton material, stuffed. Their dolls went under the name of Angelbrand, and an angel was used for their trademark.

The dolls of Kammer and Reinhardt were marked with a star between the initials K and R, and the firm of Simon and Halbig also used a star for their trademark with the initials S and H. They specialized in the making of dolls' heads. The initials F.G. mark a doll made by Ferdinand Gautier.

In 1877, wax dolls made entirely in wax were manufactured by Weisenthal Schindel and Kaltenburg, at Waltershausen, these usually being baby dolls.

Porcelain heads came from Bavaria, Prussia and from Austria. Because of import duties, the fronts of these heads were hollowed out. Painted dolls' heads came from Sonneberg and Coburg. Dolls' heads from cardboard were made by Voit of Hildburghausen. Ernest Heubach is another well-known maker.

Little German penny dolls were familiar between the years 1888 and 1908.

Germany exhibited dolls at the French Exhibitions, and in 1851, J. V. Albert was mentioned for his dolls. The town of Hamburg had many doll-makers living there, and dolls of papier-mâché, and of wax, were sent to the exhibitions. Dolls both dressed and undressed came from Prussia. Many of these were exported to England, but the country of their origin was often not marked until after the year 1890, when a law came into force making this necessary.

Simon and Halbig are well known for their fine bisque dolls, and well-known names of the 20th century are those of Käthe Kruse, Marian Kaulitz, Lotte Pritzel and Hummel. The Kruse dolls, made of felt, are unbreakable and lifelike, with often real hair, and nowadays washable faces. The Kaulitz ones are childlike, and the Pritzel dolls are more sophisticated and grown-up. The Hummel dolls are of rubber, hand-painted and made from sketches drawn by a German nun.

Hand-carved dolls are made in Berchtesgaden, and all around the villages of the Black Forest are carved toys and dolls. The Bavarian National Museum in Munich has a collection of Christmas cribs, and in Nuremberg is a collection of dolls' houses from A.D. 1639.

The celluloid doll in Swiss costume on page 115 may be one made by the German firm of Schultzmarke.

J. D. Kestner. 1896
Dolls with kid bodies and bisque heads

Back of doll which says 'Ah ah' when bent over.

Pedigree doll

Dolls made by Kammer and Reinhardt

About 1921, Lenzi dolls from Italy, made of felt and pressed, were popular and were given away as spot-prizes at dances in hotels, such as in Bournemouth, England. Dressed as shepherdesses, with full skirts and ribbons, they were not playthings but decorations, and were left lying about on sofas and settees.

Some of these decorative dolls may have coloured nails, but prior to 1786, nail varnish was unknown in England although, by 1880, fashionable women would tint their fingernails. In about 1928, long red fingernails were the fashion in Paris and, by 1932, coloured nails were the thing in America, and in England about 1933. In 1939, many people also coloured their toe nails.

In Pollock's Toy Museum, London, there is an Armand-Marseille doll with red fingernails. She is dressed in the traditional costermonger costume of a 'Pearly Princess', by the Pearly Queen of Lambeth, Mrs Lily Lodge. Many of the plastic dolls of today have red fingernails.

'Dolly-mops' may still be found in a shop in the Farringdon Road, near Ludgate Circus, London. These are dishclothes, dusters, pegs, etc. all carefully draped around a washing-up mop, which is used as the hair, and a wooden spoon for a face. These smiling dolls could come under the heading of what is known as 'Popular Art'. This year, 1960, they are known as 'Tidy-girls'.

DRGM 160633

Sign on doll, page 119 The letters DRGM stand for DEUTSCHES-REICHSGEBRAUCHSMUSTER meaning a German Registered Design.

Victor Tuckman & Co.,
Invicta Works,
Toys and Dolls. 1891

Leopold Emil Jacob,
London Wall.
Importer of Toys in 1893

FS&C
1253
39

TRADE MARK REGISTERED
MARQUE DE FABRIQUE DÉPOSÉE
GARANTIE DE QUALITE
SUPÉRIEURE

Heinrich Handwerck
in Walterhausen
Germany

Elizabeth Horne, who proposes
to carry on business under the style
of the Real Doll's House, Female Toy
Making Depot, 9 Greencroft Gardens,
South Hampstead, Middlesex.
Wife of Frederick Horne. 1890. Toys,
but not including Dolls' Houses

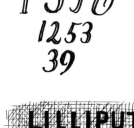

LILLIPUT

Emil Thurnauer,
Albert Dürer Strasse, Nuremberg
Wood and papier-mâché toys. 1899

Modern dolls are made from numerous kinds of plastic, and many are made from material known as vinyl. The International Aviation Co. makes dolls under the name of Pedigree dolls. In *A Book of Dolls* there is a drawing of a doll made in 1953, which says 'Aah' when bent over.

A modern doll of about 16 inches high made by this firm has a face of 3 inches high to the hair, which shows the present-day trend of making the heads large in proportion to the body. Some of these dolls are washable, including the hair, and one with socks and shoes costs about 45s.

Another make of doll is the 'Rosebud', but there are many firms and many materials, and different prices. An unbreakable vinyl doll, with nylon-clad legs, will cost as much as 9 guineas – one dressed as a bride will be 3 guineas, and most of them have nylon hair. Costume dolls can be found in many shops – Chinese rag dolls in authentic costumes cost £1 7s. 6d., and smaller ones can be had for 5s. each.

The Horsman dolls made at Trenton, in New Jersey, U.S.A., have well-made childlike faces. The heads are of vinyl plastic and the wigs are made of synthetic fibres, some with straight hair, some with curly, and all can be styled according to the fashion of an 'up-to-the-minute' child.

Kachina dolls can be seen in the Museum of the American Indian, in New York, and dolls of every size and fashion, including Jenny Lind paper dolls, are in the Museum of the City of New York. The Brooklyn Museum has a shop where modern dolls of all kinds from many countries may be purchased, and there are also dolls for sale in the United Nations building.

We do not sell dolls in museums in London, as the custom is in New York, but with a little hunting, many handmade dolls can be found in the streets around Mayfair, and in some of the Stores.

The Yugoslav travel and handicraft shop in Regent Street, London, has beautiful handmade stuffed dolls in authentic peasant dress, small ones about 10s. 6d., up to larger ones of 25s. each, and pairs of dolls, a man and a woman, for 6 guineas the pair, complete in a box and wearing traditional clothes.

The large shops all have beautiful dolls for children, English dolls and costume dolls, and many of the latter can be purchased in the handicraft shops in London, mostly round about Regent Street and Oxford Street, which still seems to be a centre for dolls since the days of the Montanaris and the Pierottis and other famous doll-makers.

Inside are all manner of things for dolls, just as there are for real children. All kinds of dresses, party frocks, bathing dresses, duffle coats, socks and shoes, and wooden or plastic coat hangers for their wardrobes, even clothes for the 'Teen-age' doll. It seems to be the age for 'off-the-peg' clothes, and does not encourage a small girl to sew, or 'thus to acquire the use of the needle'.

Paper doll with changeable dresses by A. Tuck. 1893

Year	Name	Description	Origin	Number
1820		Eyes of enamelled glass or painted china, brown, violet and sapphire.	England	
1823	DOLLS AT THE INDUSTRIAL EXHIBITION		France	
1824	Maelzel	Speaking doll, says 'Papa' and 'Mama' in English.	France	
1825		The earliest known sleeping-doll, lever for opening and closing eyes came out at the waist.		
1827	Maelzel	Patents his doll.		
1830	C. & H. White Milton, Hampshire	Make Pedlar dolls.	England	
1830	Biedermeyer type dolls	Hair is put on to a small spot of black on crown of head. The originals had cloth bodies and china arms and legs. Biedermeyer period lasts from 1835–40.	Germany	
1831		*American Girls' Book* gives directions for a Common Linen Doll.	U.S.A.	
1839	Goodyear	Rubber dolls.	U.S.A.	
1840		Papier-mâché heads with wax-coated faces, painted eyebrows, lashes, lips and cheeks.	England	
1840		Leather dolls with china heads, Sonneberg.	Germany	
1840		Wax dolls with moulded hair. 1840 – 1845	England	
1843	Petit	China doll.	France	1.62p489
1844	Thomas Forster	Improvements in preparing compositions of india-rubber and other matters, in order to make articles by casting moulds, such as balls, legs, arms, heads or other parts of dolls or figures. India-rubber, shellac, gum-opal, asphaltum and arseniate of potash.	England	10,092
1844	Monsieur Jumeau	Shows dolls at the Industries Fair.	France	
1844	Monsieur Belton Salle au Comte St.	Shows dolls at the Industries Fair.	France	
1844	Monsieur Brouillet 116 Saint Denis St.	Makes well-dressed dolls.	France	
1849	Augusta Montanari	Makes wax dolls.	England	
1849	Napoleon Montanari	Makes children's toys and wax figures.	England	
1849	John Edward Payne	India-rubber and certain gums. Gutta-percha in the manufacture of dolls. Moulding and joining a hollow figure. A piece of the compound is boiled until it is in a soft state; it is then ready for the mould. The mould for each figure consists of a front mould, a front core, a back mould and a back core. The moulds are made to act upon the material by means of pressure. In joining the shells thus formed, a red hot heater for an Italian iron is employed to the edges or rims of the said shells, they, the shells, are then pressed together and trimmed. The compound is made of gutta-percha, chopped fine, masticated in water, containing salt and oil of vitriol, and boiled, pressed, brushed, hammered and rolled.	England	12,643
1850		Sewing machine invented.		
1850		Limbed baby dolls come to England from Germany. The papier-mâché is dipped in wax and looks like real skin.	England	
1850	Huret	Dolls.	France	11,18p250 11,41p354

Between 1850 & 1887 a dagger indicates a wholesale doll manufacturer.

Year	Name	Description	Origin	Number
1851	THE GREAT EXHIBITION IN HYDE PARK, LONDON,		England	
1851	Madame Augusta Montanari wins medals for her wax dolls.		England	
1851	Monsieur P. Jumeau, wins medals for dolls' dresses.		England	

Year	Name	Description	Origin	Number
1852	Monsieur Arnaud	A jointed doll.	Paris	
1852	Monsieur Arnaud	Jointed dolls and also in 1864.	Paris	
1852	Antoni Bazzoni	Maker of wax dolls till 1868.	England	
1852	Mr Poole	Makes wooden dolls.	England	
1852	Moses Poole	Sculpts marble and stone, and makes boots, shoes and clogs.	England	
1852	J. Robins	Makes dolls.	England	
1852	W. Wicks	Composition dolls.	England	
1853	J. Barton	Makes wax dolls.	England	
1853	NEW YORK WORLD'S FAIR			
1854	H. Pierotti	Wax doll-maker.	England	
1854	Jean Baptiste André Quinquandon	Makes a machine, giving cork powder as a refuse, used for stuffing dolls.	England	2517
1854	Edouard Guichard	Improving the surface of dolls, by means of flock, applied to the surface with gums.		1455
1855	THE INTERNATIONAL EXHIBITION, PARIS			
1855	Monsieur Greffier	Makes baby dolls of low price, known as the 'Japonese' type.	France	
1855	Jumeau	Blonde bisque dolls, with the colouring applied and fired in.	France	
1855	Monsieur Blampoix	Enamelled eyes.	France	11,43p345
1855	German baby dolls shown at the Paris World Exhibition.			
1855	Augusta Montanari	Shows wax dolls.	France	
1855	Richard Napoleon Montanari	Wax with fine muslin.	England	
1855	Mr Walker	Rag doll, pattern printed on cream-coloured sateen with two little curls in front of each ear.	U.S.A.	
1855	Mr Voit of Hildburghausen	Makes dolls' heads of cardboard, with the hair dressed with taste.	Germany	
1855		Wigs glued to parian-ware heads, and clear tough wax, with the features painted before waxing.		
1856	Delphieu	Dolls.	France	11,58p30
1856	Joel Ellis	First commercial wooden doll.	U.S.A.	
1857	Monsieur Roy	Bust joints.	France	11,60p120 70941
1857	Rohmer	Leather arms.	France	1164,p295
1858	Rohmer	Doll's head.	France	1167,p179
1858	Anton Benda	Separate limbs, joined by india-rubber or other elastic strings or cords, preferably placed in the interior of the figures.	England	2283
1858	J. Luis	Drawers for dolls are constructed with pleated upper parts, enclosing springs, thus dispensing with the use of crinolines.	England	2683
1858	Herbillon	Doll.	France	1165,p289
1858	d'Autremont	India-rubber dolls.	France	1168,p299
1858	Hammond	Mechanical dolls.	France	1168,p314
1858	Richard A. Brooman	Forming dolls from vulcanized caoutchouc. Improvements in the manufacture of dolls, toys, etc. A metal mould, hermetically sealed, with a ball of caoutchouc inside and locked in the mould. Plunged in vulcanizing composition, enough for a doll, and expands with heat. The doll is in two parts, top half and bottom half, and the joins covered with a belt.	England	2639
1859	Charles Sylvester Rostaing	Improvement of using gutta-percha. A mixture of gutta-percha and other substances, so hard that it replaces wood, and can be diversely coloured. Used for skates, chess-men and doll's heads.	England	2962

Year	Name	Description	Origin	Number
1860	Izannah F. Walker	Rag doll.	U.S.A.	
1860	Monsieur Jumeau	Swivel necks.	France	
1860	M. Reidemester	Doll.	France	1178,p241
1860	Albert Haas	Improvement on dolls.	England	1866
	Fischer Naumann & Co. of Saxe Weimar	Dolls hitherto made have never been so constructed as to allow of their being placed in a sitting posture with the legs bending at and hanging down from the knee . . . in the position of a living person.		
1860	Galibert	Moving doll.	France	1175,p224
1860	Herland	Musical and jumping dolls.	France	68122
1860	Lechertier Barbe	Paper doll.	France	79722
1860	Poncet	Paper doll.	France	
1860	Brouillet			
	Cacheleux	Paste-board doll.	France	1178,p271
	Briens	Doll.	France	1178,p188
1860	Darizard	Doll's head.	France	1173,p421
1861	William Clark	A walking doll.	England	1664
1861	Bertal & Taffre	Historical doll.	France	181c20p2
1861	H. Pierotti	Inventor of the Royal Model dolls.	England	
1861	Chauvière	Doll.	France	1181c20p3
1861	C. Stevens	Gutta-percha or india-rubber animals and dolls coated with glue, then with natural skin.	England	1146
1861	W. Clark	Doll, step by step movement, resembling walking.	England	1664
1862	INTERNATIONAL EXHIBITION, LONDON			
1862	Alfred Vincent Newton	Mechanical Doll, 1862, U.S.A. Letters patent to Alfred Vincent Newton. A communication from abroad by Enoch Rice Morrison, of New York City, United States of America. Sealed the 5th May 1863, and dated the 20th December, 1862. 'This invention relates to the construction and peculiar arrangement of double eccentric cams, joints in connection with vertical or upright levers and pedal supports . . . by suitable clock mechanism the figure will be propelled along silently by a stepping movement. . . . It is particularly adapted for dolls, and also for quadrupeds of various kinds, such as the elephant, camel, horse, ox, sheep, dogs, etc., to give them locomotion which is lifelike in appearance. . . . It will greatly contribute to the amusement of children and not a little to adults.' British Specification, No. 3408. Picture on page 2.	U.S.A.	
1862	Pierotti wins bronze medal at the International Exhibition.			
1862	Steiner	Speaking doll.	France	1183c20 p20
1862	Briens	Jointed doll.	France	1183c20 p18
1862	Souty	Pumice stone.	France	1183c20 p26
1862	Jean Mougin	Barcelonnettes, cradles for children and dolls.	England	
1863	Lamour	Automaton doll.	France	
1863	Munn & Cobb	Automatic walking doll.	England	
1863	Steiner	Mechanical doll.	France	57863
1863		The Autoperipatetikos Doll patented in U.S.A.		
1864	Marcus Brown-Westhead	Dancing Toys. A walking doll.	England	61
1864	Lacoruchy	Doll.	France	1190 64256te

Year	Name	Description	Origin	Number
1864	Monsieur Arnaud	A jointed doll, the mechanism is composed of concave and convex parts, which are brought and pressed together, and held by rubber etc.	France	61809
1864		Jointed doll, walking down a plank.	England	
1865	John Longbottom	Dolls from a composition called Kampakaon.	England	1775
1865	Anquelle	Doll.	France	1194
				68136te
1865	Egrefeuil	Doll in a box.	France	1194
				67276te
1865	W. Clark	Composition for making dolls' heads: glue 4 lb., Nutgall etc. 3 oz., glycerine 8 oz., acid 1 lb.		
1866	David Lee	Joints or other moving parts, connected by springs, the joints being formed upon the ball and socket principle, so that they can move in any direction, and stay by the action of the springs.	England	1579
1866	J. S. Cavell	Dancing doll.		
1866	John Pepper	Gymnastic figures.	England	
1866	Clement	Leather doll.	France	70283
1866	Lecomet-Alliot	Doll.	France	73992
1867	INTERNATIONAL EXHIBITION, PARIS			
1867	T. C. Clarkson	Dolls of West Indian cork.		
1867	Monsieur Bru	Doll with turning head, showing two expressions, one crying.	France	78844
1867	Joliet	Jointed doll.	France	76520
1868	Hawkins	Moulded doll.	France	83285
1868	Chamson	Doll of paste.	France	83211
1868	John Edwards	Exhibition dolls, of wax, rag, composition, dressed or undressed.	England	
1868	Bès	Doll.	France	83361
1868	Cavell	Doll.	France	79581
1869	Madame Restignat	A jointed doll made of cork.	France	84707
1869	Boutard	A flying doll.	France	87264
1869	Damas-Lajon	Holder for a doll.	France	85644
1869	Leverd et Cie	Jointed doll.	France	85557
1869	Jules Nicolas Steiner	Toy manufacturer, velocipedes and automatic toys. 25 Rue de Saintonge.	France	2729
1869	Chavallier et Brasseur	Doll of artificial wood.	France	80827
1869	Monsieur Bru	Second patent for perfecting the manufacture of dolls.	France	64302
1870	E. Moody sells dolls in the Soho Bazaar, London.		England	
1870	Chauvière	A speaking doll.	France	88653
1870	H. J. Meech, 50 Wilmington Rd, London, S.E.	Doll-maker to the Royal Family from this date onwards. Name stamped on calico body.	England	
1871	Parent	Jointed doll.	France	1112c20p7
1871	L'Hotte	Doll.	France	111.11.ic
1871	Franklin	A wax doll with this name is in Kensington Palace.		20p15
1872	Madame Bru	Magical doll, a talking doll, which sang various airs.	France	1114c20p17
1872	Pannier	Dolls with metallic frames and joints.	France	
1872	Benda	Dolls' head.	France	1114c20p20
1872	Gauthier	Dolls' head.	France	
1872	Clarke, Nicholls & Coombe make little figures of sweets, about this time.		England	
1872	Joel Ellis	Lead or pewter hands and feet.	U.S.A.	
1873	INTERNATIONAL EXHIBITION, VIENNA			
1873	Izannah F. Walker	Manufacturer of dolls, the originator of America's first commercial wooden doll.	U.S.A.	144,373

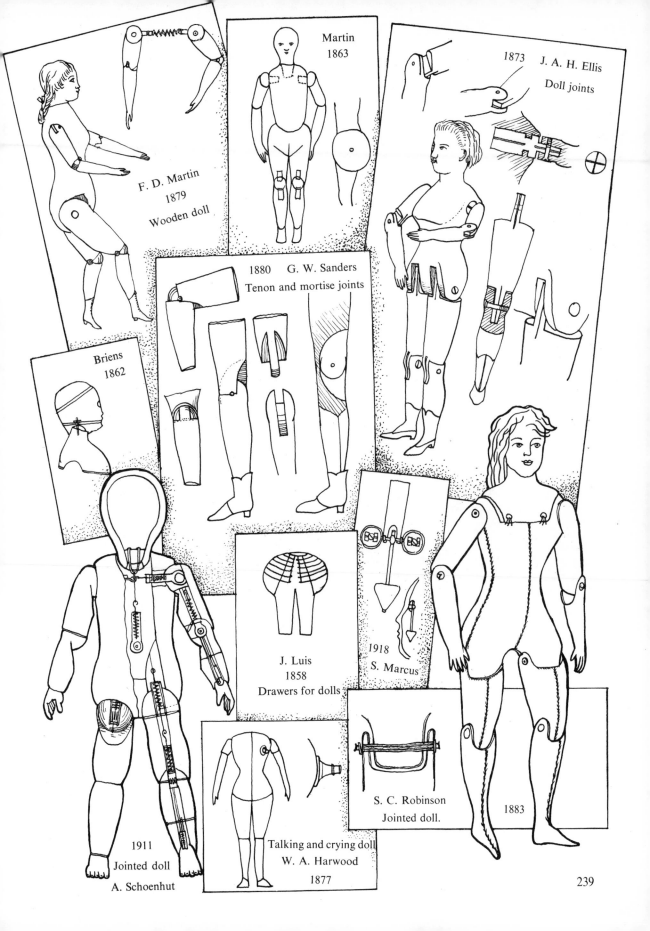

F. D. Martin
1879
Wooden doll

Martin
1863

1873   J. A. H. Ellis
Doll joints

1880   G. W. Sanders
Tenon and mortise joints

Briens
1862

J. Luis
1858
Drawers for dolls

1918
S. Marcus

1911
Jointed doll
A. Schoenhut

Talking and crying doll
W. A. Harwood
1877

S. C. Robinson
Jointed doll.

1883

239

Year	Name	Description	Origin	Number
1873	J. A. H. Ellis	Doll joints. This is for a wooden doll. It is said that all Ellis dolls have black feet, and all Springfield dolls have blue ones.	U.S.A.	139,130
1873	A. Walker	Stuffed doll, material pressed with glue.	U.S.A.	
1874	Gerardin	Movable caoutchouc doll.	France	
1874	Gerarbon	A grimacing doll.	France	111ii,ic 20p9
1874	W. H. Hart	Doll.	U.S.A.	157,394
1874	A. W. Monroe	Doll, with natural hair and adjusting head, hard rubber and Angora goat hair. He claims to be the first to make a hard rubber doll, ball-shaped head, resting in socket, secured by elastic band. Wig of the natural pelt of the Angora goat.	U.S.A.	159437
1875		In America the wooden doll industry centred on Springfield, Vermont.		
1875	W. Miller	Rubber doll, with flexible wire inside it.	U.S.A.	164582
1875	A. E. Hotchkiss	A clockwork walking doll.	U.S.A.	167899
1875	Schmetzer	Dancing doll.	France	111fe
1876	PHILADELPHIA CENTENNIAL EXHIBITION			
1876	Vervelle	A metallic doll.	France	115279
1876	Martin	Swimming doll.	France	115897
1876	Bourrillon	Doll.	France	11,19iic 20p42 115615te
1877	W. A. Harwood	Talking and crying doll, by means of blowing through a tube.	U.S.A.	189.935
1877	About this time, London imports glass eyes for dolls from Germany.			
1878	T. A. Edison	Phonograph dolls, the lips of the mask move.	England	
1878	INTERNATIONAL EXHIBITION, PARIS			
1879	F. D. Martin	Wooden dolls with socket and ball joints, with elastic or spiral springs.	U.S.A.	214830
1879	Charles Marsh, 114 Fulham Rd, London	Wax dolls, over a papier-mâché foundation	England	
1880	G. W. Sanders	Tenon and mortise joints for dolls.	U.S.A.	235,300
1880	W. B. Carpenter	A method of colouring the eyebrows of celluloid dolls. Use of pumice-stone in finishing dolls' heads, eyebrows incised and coloured before pumicing. 'I claim a most beautiful and natural look.'	U.S.A U.S.A.	235,933 237,599
1880	C. T. Dotter	Doll with corsets.	U.S.A.	235,218
1880	Simon & Halbig	The best makers of German bisque dolls.	Germany	
1880	Simon & Halbig	Doll's eyes.	Germany	
1880	H. Pierotti	Makes dolls and has a shop in Oxford Street, known as London Crystal Palace Gallery.	England	
1881	Mason & Taylor	Construction of dolls. A turning head.	U.S.A.	242,210
1881	Bartenstein	Doll's head. A German movable double face. Laughing on one side, crying on the other.	U.S.A.	243,752
1881	Bartenstein	Doll's head.	Germany	
1882	C. C. Johnson	Doll's head. An improved head covered with plastic	U.S.A.	267,212
1883	S. C. Robinson	Jointed doll.	U.S.A.	283,513
1883	Martha Wellington	Makes rag dolls.	U.S.A.	
1884	Webber	Singing doll, when squeezed will sing patriotic songs.	U.S.A.	
1885	P. Goldsmith	Doll-body with corsets, body made of kid or cloth, with an imported German china head.	U.S.A.	
1885		Up to 1885, all American rag dolls were made at home.		

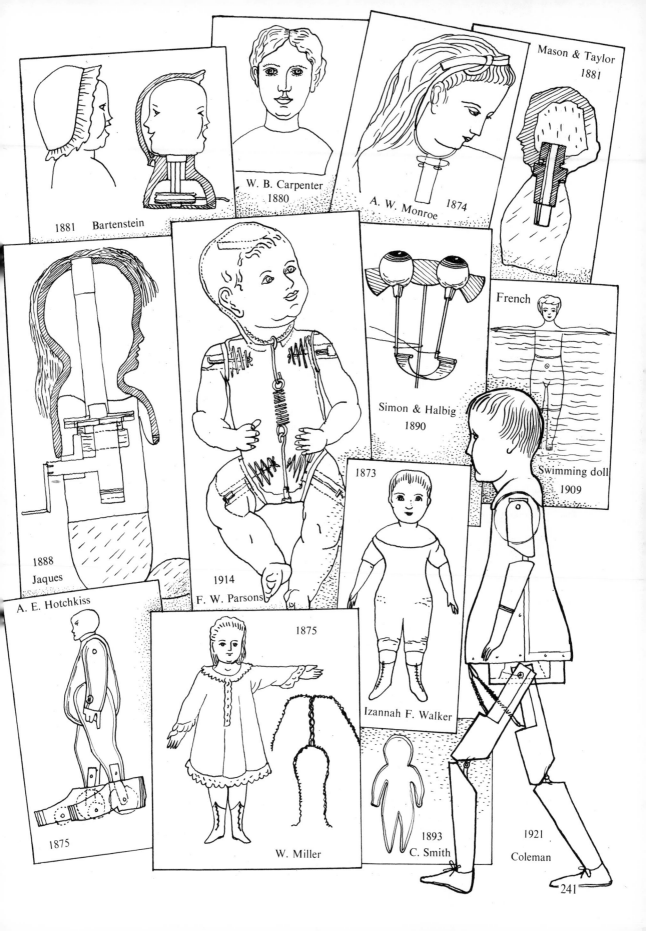

1881 Bartenstein

W. B. Carpenter
1880

A. W. Monroe 1874

Mason & Taylor
1881

1888
Jaques

Simon & Halbig
1890

French

Swimming doll
1909

1873

1914
F. W. Parsons

Izannah F. Walker

A. E. Hotchkiss

1875

1875

W. Miller

1893
C. Smith

1921
Coleman

Year	Name	Description	Origin	Number
1885	THE INTERNATIONAL PARIS EXHIBITION			
1885	Madame Montanari	Shows dolls.	France	
1885	Napoleon Montanari	Shows statuettes and figurines in wax.	France	
1885	Richard Napoleon Montanari	Shows wax dolls coated with fine muslin.	France	
1888	Jaques	A talking doll, a doll combined with a phonograph.	U.S.A.	383299
1889	Rudolf Steiner	Dolls.	England	14534
1889	J. C. Morrell	Games. Crawling dolls.	England	
1890	Monsieur Jumeau	A bisque doll, with phonograph in chest, so that it alters the conversation.	France	
1890	Josef Bayer writes the *Puppenfee Ballet*, about a fairy doll.			
1890	THE TARIFF ACT, IN WHICH EVERY DOLL HAD TO BE MARKED WITH ITS PLACE OF ORIGIN.			
1891	Meech	Makes dolls for the Royal Family.	England	
1893	C. Smith	Makes rag dolls from two pieces, with darts and gussets.	England	
1893	A. Tuck	Dolls printed in colours, upon cardboard, with a number of changeable dresses.	England	23.003
1893	A. J. Boult	Doll with metal rods inside and a marble. As the doll is moved about, musical sounds are produced.	England	
1893	I. A. Gutsell	Doll.	U.S.A.	503,313
1894	Morrell, 368 Oxford St, London. Makes dolls.		England	
1895	W. T. Jefferson	Paper doll.	U.S.A.	535,621
1895	Johann Heinrich	Toy figures made in pewter and lead, Bavaria.	Germany	
1895	Mary Ann Marsh	Takes over the shop in the Fulham Road, London.	England	
1896	Kestner	Dolls with kid bodies and bisque heads.	U.S.A.	
1896	Kestner, junior	The company which later made the first Kewpies of America. In England, these were little naked celluloid dolls with two blue wings at the back of the neck.	U.S.A.	
1897	E. T. Gibson	Toy paper doll.	U.S.A.	585,092
1898	S. Marsh	His patent on dolls was withdrawn and not published.	England	9480
1898	Monsieur Jumeau and Monsieur Bru join with others to form a society for the manufacture of dolls.			
1898	J. B. Sheppard	Stockinette doll.	U.S.A.	
1899	Mrs Twiss, awarded the Gold Medal for 'Princess Daisy' at the International Exhibition at Amsterdam.			
1900	M. L. Mead	Rag doll.	U.S.A.	661,185
1900	E. G. Newell	Toy doll.	U.S.A.	643,385
1900	Thomas Betts	Dolls.	England	
1902	Lucy Peck	Wax dolls with inset hair	England	
1902	Steiner	Walking doll.	U.S.A.	695,121
1903	Dean's Rag Book Co.	A big baby doll, printed on a linen sheet 30 in. by 28 in. with directions for stuffing and making up, printed in three languages.	England	
1903	Harrison	Paper doll.		
1903	Frederick Bosworth	He makes fashion dolls at 9 New Burlington Street, London.	England	
1904	Kate Reilly Ltd	Fashion dolls at Dover Street, London.	England	
1904	EXHIBITION AT ST. LOUIS		U.S.A.	
		Ancient dolls, caoutchouc dolls, frilly dolls with enormous hats.		
1904		The sleeping-eyed bisque heads are more expensive than the china ones. Also there are heads made of metal.	Germany	

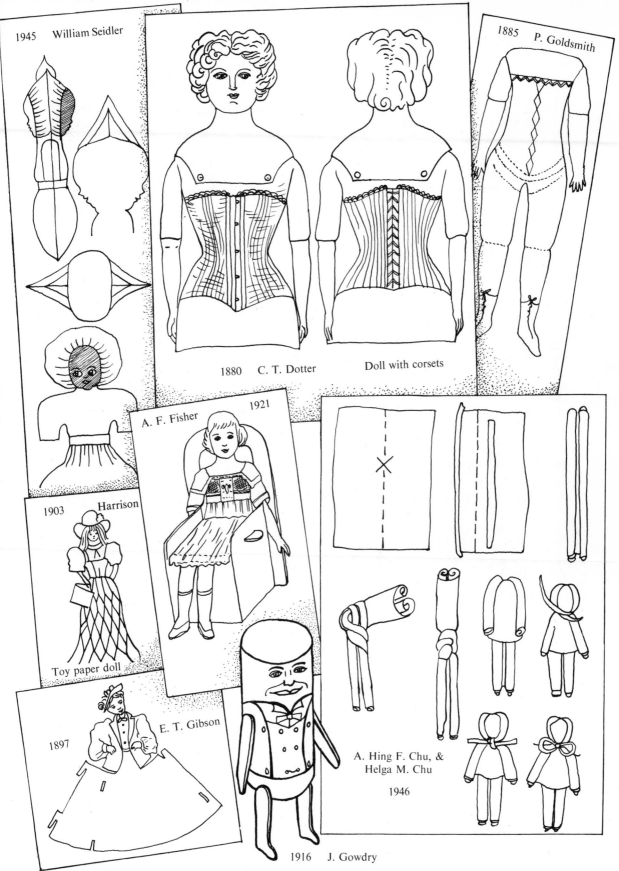

1945   William Seidler

1880   C. T. Dotter

Doll with corsets

1885   P. Goldsmith

A. F. Fisher   1921

1903   Harrison

Toy paper doll

1897   E. T. Gibson

A. Hing F. Chu, &
Helga M. Chu

1946

1916   J. Gowdry

Year	Name	Description	Origin	Number
1910	Marian Kaulitz, Munich	Porcelain dolls with simple cotton dresses.	Germany	
1911	A. Schoenhut	Jointed doll, with spring-loaded universal joints.	U.S.A.	982,096
1912	E. Horsman	Doll.	U.S.A.	42324 and 42325
1914	F. W. Parsons	Doll. A celluloid doll with joints held on by wire springs. Scraps used from making celluloid collars. The dolls float in water. These were baby dolls.	U.S.A.	1,120,331
1914	Anna Pavlova dances in New York, dressed as a doll in a costume designed by Albert Rutherston.		U.S.A.	
1914		Dolls were not manufactured in America on a large scale until World War I.		
1916	J. Gowdry	An improved tumbling doll.	U.S.A.	1,214,454
1917	Coleman	Walking doll.	U.S.A.	1,221970
1918	S. Marcus	Artificial eyes for Dolls. Hollow shells of celluloid, eyes connected as a pair, weight in centre. Eyes sold separately.	U.S.A.	1,252469
1919		Aluminium doll. This is a jointed doll, made of wood, hollow and strung with elastic. Head, hands and feet made of aluminium.	Germany	
1920		The Bye-lo baby dolls.	U.S.A.	
1921	Coleman	Another walking doll.	U.S.A.	1,396321
1921	A. F. Fisher	Sitting doll. A cardboard cut-out doll.	U.S.A.	1,369093
1921		Wooden heads with movable wooden eyes.	U.S.A.	
1941		Doll with magnetic hands to pick up and hold things.	U.S.A.	
1945	William Seidler of New York	A two-faced doll, one black and one white.	U.S.A.	2396441
1946	A. Hing F. Chu, & Helga M. Chu	A doll of folded cloth at Larchmont, N.Y.	U.S.A.	2406994
1951	FESTIVAL OF BRITAIN			

Even where the patent was not carried through, it still gives an idea of the kind of doll one can expect at that period, and it is interesting where the same kind of thing was happening in two countries far apart. The numbers after the word 'France' refer to the tomes at the Patent office, London.

Porcelain figure by Heubach. 1880
German patent No 11153
Doll by Fritz Bartenstein in Huttensteinach, Sonneberg
1881 german patent No 17327.

THE FOLLOWING EXTRACTS ARE TAKEN FROM
BOOKS IN WHICH DOLLS ARE MENTIONED

From 'Youthful Sports' 1801

But the thing that was looked forward to was Reading Great Fair. . . . . Madame . . . . used to take the children round the fair on the first day, but they had to walk two and two, and hold each other by the hand. They were not allowed to go inside the marionette-show or any of the peepshows, or ride on the giddy-go-round, that would not have been considered suitable for little ladies: but they each got sixpence to spend on a fairing. You could get balls and dolls, little china plates and mugs, big enough to drink out of, all for a halfpenny, and there was gingerbread with gilt dust on it, the best in the kingdom. All their lives Cassandra and Jane Austen would remember Reading Great Fair.

At Godmersham, in the old nursery, Edward's children had a doll's house with a pillared portico and real glass in all the windows. When Fanny or Marianne or little Louisa swung open the front you saw the whole Lilliputian establishment at once, upstairs and downstairs and in my lady's chamber, as the nursery rhyme went.

Jane, born 1774. Fanny, born 1793. *Parson Austen's Daughter*, by Helen Ashton, published by Collins

My first visit to Germany was in 1883, when I was eleven, . . . I can remember it still perfectly well: how for days before we started I was packing my little box with all the bits and pieces and also my dolls.

My Memories of Six Reigns, by Her Highness Princess Marie Louise, published by Evans Bros. of London

The Victorian Doll, who, often elaborately dressed, of finest wax and with real hair, was wrapped in tissue paper and kept in the bottom drawer of the spare-room, thence to emerge only on Sundays. I do not suggest that this custom was universal. In many houses dolls were not permitted at all on Sundays. But I have met a number of Sunday dolls – indeed possessed one myself – Nelly, her name – dressed in black silk powdered with gold flowers. Nelly had a bustle and short socks of drab knitted cotton. She possessed for me the religious significance inevitable in all dolls whose superior qualities of dress and appearance made the Sabbath afternoon, mellow with nuts and ginger wine, alone worthy of their attention.

From *The True History of Dolls*, by Muriel Harris, born about 1885

Ernest Shepherd, the artist, when he was young, played with dolls. He and his sisters would let them down from the landing in baskets. He mentions this in the book he wrote on his childhood, *Drawn from Memory*, published by Methuens

Freya Stark, the author and traveller, mentions some of her purchases in her book *Beyond Euphrates*, published by John Murray. She says that on the 7th August, 1931, when at Qazvin, 'I have bought two knives, two purses, two dolls, and 400 doses of quinine, as presents, etc.'

Our dolls were always supposed to have the most devastating diseases. I remember Susan's doll had smallpox, but I was determined to go one better, so my 'Primrose' had a sunstroke. However, I shall always feel that Susan behaved rather meanly over this master-stroke of mine. She declared that Primrose could not have had one, as people never recovered from sunstrokes. Poor Primrose was supposed to have a chill one day, and I sat her too close to the fire: her face being made of wax, the nose melted, which gave her a very unfortunate appearance.'

Victorian Days, by Lady Clodagh Anson, born 1879. Richards Press, London

I don't think anything has ever given me more intense pleasure than some of my playthings. I still remember with the deepest affection an Eskimo doll whose clothing could be put on and taken off.

A Choice of Ornaments, by Nicolas Bentley. Andre Deutsch

Dressing Dolls in 1804

My first distinct memory is of my father (Sir Edwin Lutyens) on the day of King George V's coronation, he came up to the nursery, and cut crowns out of orange peel for our dolls.

Betty, my sister, was able to play with toys of completely different sizes and species in the same game. Thus she could accommodate a large doll and a tiny lead animal in the same piece of make-believe, something which I was quite unable to do. In my games everything had to be to scale.

There was one doll in particular, called Ruthie, who had a very large trousseau, and I used to sit peacefully on the floor by the hour, day after day, dressing and undressing her.

... the Doll's House, which Father had designed for Queen Mary, was being constructed in our drawing room with the black walls. Furnishings of all sorts were arriving for it every day – linen, glass, china, books, pictures, curtains, chandeliers, wine bottles, golf-clubs, motor-cars, as well as the fittings which Father had designed. I went into the drawing room at all times to watch its progress and came to look upon it almost as my private possession. So much of the furniture was familiar to me – The bed in the Princess Royal's room was a perfect miniature of the beds Father had designed for Barbie and Ursula: the chandelier in the nursery was a copy of the one he had made for Barbie's new nursery, while the kitchen cupboards were reproductions of our own. I realized that this was the house we would have lived in if Father had been rich enough to build it for himself. It was his own dream house and because I was imbued with his taste it was my dream house too. It took no effort of imagination to see us living in it.

To Be Young, by Mary Lutyens, published by Rupert Hart-Davis

There is an interesting rhyme about dolls by Darton in a book called *The Dolls' Picnic*: the little yellow comb mentioned at the back of a doll's head would be like those on the dolls in Kensington Palace belonging to the Queen Victoria when a child. These dolls, in the rhyme, all have a picnic with the Nursery Rhyme folk.

> There were four little Dolls, who lived by themselves,
> In a very dark closet, on very high shelves.
> Two were waxen, and one was wood,
> Of Dutch extraction (one can't say 'blood').
> The fourth was stuffed with bran all through;
> She had very squat feet, turned slightly askew,
> And tight-fitting gloves of a deep pink hue.

> *

> Her locks were painted as black as ink,
> With a yellow comb at the back, I think.

> *

> Once more the Dolls themselves deposit
> On the dusty shelves of their gloomy closet;
> Resign themselves to their dreary lot,
> And, yearning no more for what they have not,
> In time they forget – that they are forgot!

'A very large wax doll': 1824

* * *

'Grandmamma's gift': 1826

246

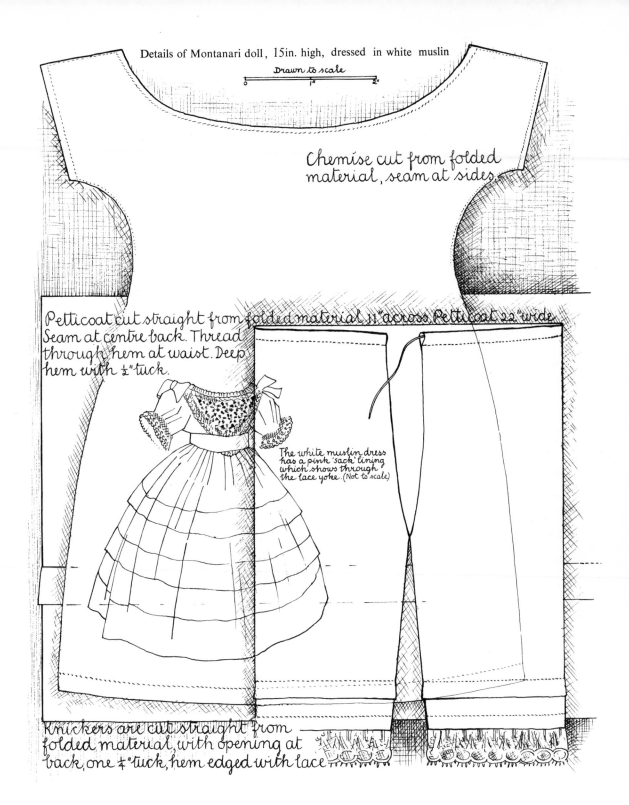

Details of Montanari doll, 15in. high, dressed in white muslin

Drawn to scale

Chemise cut from folded
material, seam at sides.

Petticoat cut straight from folded material 11"across Petticoat 22" wide
Seam at centre back. Thread
through hem at waist. Deep
hem with ½"tuck.

The white muslin dress
has a pink 'sack' lining
which shows through
the lace yoke. (Not to scale)

Knickers are cut straight from
folded material, with opening at
back, one ¾"tuck, hem edged with lace.

LIST OF MUSEUMS

There are dolls in the following museums:

ENGLAND:

Abbey House Museum, Leeds
Ashmolean Museum, Oxford
Aylesbury Museum, Buckinghamshire (*a few*)
Barnard Castle, County Durham
Bristol Folk Museum, Blaise Castle House
Castle Museum, Colchester (*a few*)
Chester Museum
Fitzwilliam Museum, Cambridge
Folk Museum, Cambridge
The Doll Museum, Warwick
Harris Museum, Preston
Helston Museum, Cornwall (*a few*)
Hollytrees Museum, Colchester
Hove Museum, Sussex
Lanhydrock House, Bodmin, Cornwall
Longford Castle, near Salisbury
Luton Museum, Bedfordshire
Pitt Rivers Museum, Oxford
Pitt Rivers Museum, Farnham Royal, Dorset
Priest's House, West Hoathly
Queens Park Art Gallery, Manchester
Red House, Christchurch, Hants
Salisbury Museum, Wiltshire
St Albans Museum, Hertfordshire
Saltwell Park Museum, Gateshead
Shibden Hall, Halifax
Somerset County Museum, Taunton
Snowshill Manor, Gloucestershire
Toy Museum, Rottingdean, Brighton
Truro Museum, Cornwall (*a few*)
Tunbridge Wells Museum
Windsor Castle, Windsor
Woburn Abbey, Bedfordshire
Worthing Museum
York Castle Museum

LONDON:

Bethnal Green Museum
British Museum
Geffrye Museum, Shoreditch
Gunnersbury Museum, Middlesex
Horniman Museum, Dulwich
Imperial Institute, South Kensington
   (*will soon be moving to Holland House*)
London Museum, Kensington Palace
Pollock's Toy Museum
Wellcome Museum, Wellcome Institute
Victoria & Albert Museum

Museum of Childhood, Edinburgh, Scotland
Royal Scottish Museum, Edinburgh
Tollcross Museum, Glasgow
Dublin Museum, Ireland
Tenby Museum, Wales (*a few*)

OVERSEAS:

Transvaal Museum, Pretoria, South Africa
National Museum of Canada, Ottawa
Bavarian National Museum, Munich
Germanic National Museum, Nuremberg
Musée des Arts Décoratifs, Paris
Musée Carnavalet, Paris
Openair Folk Museum, Arnhem
Children's Museum, Detroit
Essex Institute, Salem, Massachusetts
American Indian Museum, New York
Heye Foundation, New York
Metropolitan Museum, New York
Brooklyn Children's Museum, New York
New York City Museum
Nordiska Museet, Stockholm
United Nations Building, New York
Van Cortlandt House Museum, New York

More about dolls can be found in the following books:

Children's Toys of Bygone Days, Karl Grober
Dolls and Puppets, Max von Boehn
Puppen aus Aller Welt, Claus Hansmann
Ancient and Modern Dolls, Gwen White
A Book of Dolls, Gwen White
English Dolls, Effigies and Puppets, Alice K. Earley
Peepshow into Paradise, Lesley Gordon
Fascinating Story of Dolls, Janet P. Johl
More About Dolls, Janet P. Johl
Dolls of Yesterday, Eleanor St George
Dolls of Three Centuries, Eleanor St George
American Dolls, Ruth Freeman
Guide for Collectors, Clare Fawcett

BOOKS to which reference has been made:

By Eskimo Dog-sled, S. K. Hutton
Among the Eskimos of Labrador, S. K. Hutton
The Thlingets of Alaska, Livingston Jones
The Aztecs of Mexico, G. C. Vaillant
Games, Walter Hough
Primitive Art, Leonard Adam
The National Geographical Magazine, U.S.A.
Mélanges Africanistes, Jean Paul Lebeuf
The Ila-speaking People, the Rev. Edwin Smith
Pygmies and Bushmen of the Kalahari, S. S. Dorman
The Spirit-ridden Konde, D. R. Mackenzie
Nuer Customs, Huffman
Modern Egyptians, E. W. Lane
History of the Egyptian People, Walter Budge
Ashanti, Captain R. S. Rattray
Bull. Ifan. 2, jan-avr. 1940, Mamadou Traore
Africa, E. Lovett
Decoration of Negro Graves, E. Ingersoll
Mayhew's London, 1851
The Doll's Picnic, Darton
Unter den Natur Völkern Zentral-Brasiliens, Berlin, K. von den Steinen
Zeitschrift für Ethnologie, 1910, Heft 3 & 4, E. Nordenskiöld
Ymer, 1910, 2 livraison
Persian Women, Colliver Rice
Peasant Life in the Holy Land, Wilson
The Pampas and the Andes, W. T. Blake
Lenguan Indians, Paraguayan Chaco, Barbrooke Grubb
La vie des Indiens dans le Chaco (Revue de Geographie), E. Nordenskiöld
The New Zealand Aborigines, William Brown
Pounamu, the New Zealand Greenstone, Maj. Gen. H. G. Robley
The Melanesians, Codrington
The Mafulu People of the British New Guinea, Robert Williamson
Natives of Australia, N. W. Thomas, M.A.
The Australian Aboriginal, Herbert Basedon
Seventeen Years among the Dyaks of Borneo, Edwin Gomes
Native Dolls in the Transvaal Museum, A. Radcliffe Brown
Jeux et Jouets, Leo Claretie
Histoire des Jouets, Henri d'Allemagne
The Trade Marks Journal

ACKNOWLEDGEMENTS

I wish to thank the following for their help:

British Museum Library
Australia House Library
International African Library
Wellcome Museum Library
Hertfordshire County Library
Victoria & Albert Museum Library
Patent Office Library
Archives Department, Westminster
Westminster Reference Library
South American Missionary Society
Church Missionary Society
Trustees of the London Museum
Horniman Museum, Dulwich
Miss Muriel Pierotti
Dean's Rag Book Co. Ltd
Cauldron Potteries, Stoke-on-Trent
Transvaal Museum
Bethnal Green Museum
Luton Museum, Bedfordshire
Openair Folk Museum, Arnhem

and all the missionaries, explorers, and collectors who have brought dolls back with them on their travels, and all the young ladies who have lent me their dolls from which to make portraits.

G.B.W.

The material and extracts from Patent Specifications are by kind permission of the Controller of H.M. Stationery Office.

INDEX

Page numbers in heavy type denote illustration

Shell figure from Antigua   Made by J. N. Walter

one |————| ½ inch

The doll from Ireland
waves goodbye